Elements of
Language
Introductory
Course

Spelling
Lessons and Activities

- **Word Lists**
- **Instruction**
- **Practice**

D1299837

HOLT, RINEHART AND WINSTON

A Harcourt Classroom Education Company

Austin · New York · Orlando · Atlanta · San Francisco · Boston · Dallas · Toronto · London

EDITORIAL

Director

Mescal Evler

Ma...ns

Bill Wahlgren

Executive Editor

Emily G. Shenk

Project Editor

James E. Eckel

Writing and Editing:

Karen S. Ellis, Michael Nassoiy

Editorial Assistant:

Kim Soriano

Copyediting:

Michael Neibergall, *Copyediting Manager;* Mary Malone, *Senior Copyeditor;* Joel Bourgeois, Elizabeth Dickson, Gabrielle Field, Jane Kominek, Millicent Ondras, Theresa Reding, Kathleen Scheiner, Laurie Schlesinger, *Copyeditors*

Project Administration:

Marie Price, *Managing Editor;* Lori De La Garza, *Editorial Operations Coordinator;* Thomas Browne, Heather Cheyne, Diane Hardin, Mark Holland, Marcus Johnson, Jill O'Neal, Joyce Rector, Janet Riley, Kelly Tankersley, *Project Administration;* Gail Coupland, Ruth Hooker, Margaret Sanchez, *Word Processing*

Editorial Permissions:

Janet Harrington, *Permissions Editor*

ART, DESIGN AND PHOTO

Graphic Services

Kristen Darby, *Manager*

Image Acquisitions

Joe London, *Director;* Tim Taylor, *Photo Research Supervisor;* Rick Benavides, *Assistant Photo Researcher;* Elaine Tate, *Supervisor;* Erin Cone, *Art Buyer*

Cover Design

Sunday Patterson

PRODUCTION

Belinda Barbosa Lopez, *Senior Production Coordinator* Simira Davis, *Supervisor* Nancy Hargis, *Media Production Supervisor* Joan Lindsay, *Production Coordinator* Beth Prevelige, *Prepress Manager*

MANUFACTURING

Michael Roche, *Supervisor of Inventory and Manufacturing*

Table of Contents

How to Study a Word   v

Spelling Strategies   vi

Proofreading Strategies   vii

How to Make Your Personal Word Log   viii

UNIT 1

Lesson 1	Short Vowels	1
Lesson 2	Long Vowels	2
Lesson 3	Variant Vowels	4
Lesson 4	Vowels Before *r*	6

Unit 1 Review   8
  Practice Test A
  Practice Test B
  Activities

UNIT 2

Lesson 6	Other Vowel Spellings	12
Lesson 7	Words with *ie* and *ei*	14
Lesson 8	Compound Words	16
Lesson 9	Homophones	18
Lesson 10	Easily Confused Words	20

Unit 2 Review   22
  Practice Test A
  Practice Test B
  Activities

UNIT 3

Lesson 12	Changing *y* to *i*	26
Lesson 13	Unstressed Endings /ər/, /əl/, /ən/	28
Lesson 14	Spelling Patterns—VC/CV Words	30
Lesson 15	Spelling Patterns—V/CV Words	32
Lesson 16	Adding *-ed* and *-ing*	34

Unit 3 Review   36
  Practice Test A
  Practice Test B
  Activities

UNIT 4

Lesson 18	Noun Suffix -ance / -ence	40
Lesson 19	Noun Suffixes -ship, -ment, -ity	42
Lesson 20	Prefix ad- (ac-, as-, af-, ap-)	44
Lesson 21	Prefix com- (con-)	46
Lesson 22	Unstressed Ending -ant / -ent	48

Unit 4 Review   50
  Practice Test A
  Practice Test B
  Activities

UNIT 5

Lesson 24	Spelling Patterns—More VCV Words	54
Lesson 25	Mixed Spelling Patterns	56
Lesson 26	Unusual Plurals	58
Lesson 27	Adjective Suffixes -ive, -ous	60
Lesson 28	Words with Prefixes and Suffixes	62

Unit 5 Review   64
  Practice Test A
  Practice Test B
  Activities

UNIT 6

Lesson 30	Suffixes in Combination	68
Lesson 31	Prefix in- (im-, il-, ir-)	70
Lesson 32	Latin Roots -scrib- / -script-, -spect-	72
Lesson 33	Latin Roots -rupt-, -ject-	74

Unit 6 Review   76
  Practice Test A
  Practice Test B
  Activities

Spelling Dictionary   80
Your Word Logs   105

How to Study a Word

1 SAY the word.

Remember when you have heard the word used.
Think about what it means.

2 LOOK at the word.

Find any prefixes, suffixes, or other word parts you know.
Think about other words that are related in meaning and
spelling. Try to picture the word in your mind.

3 SPELL the word to yourself.

Think about the way each sound is spelled. Notice any
unusual spelling.

**4 WRITE the word while you are
looking at it.**

Check the way you have formed your letters. If you have not
written the word clearly or correctly, write it again.

5 CHECK what you learned.

Cover the word and write it. If you did not spell the word
correctly, practice these steps until you can write it correctly
every time.

Lesson Word Log

Look in the back of this book, starting on page
106. This is where you'll list the words that you
need to study from each lesson. Include words
you miss on the pretest and any other words
you aren't sure you can always spell correctly.

Spelling Strategies

Here are some helpful spelling strategies. Think about them as you come across words you don't know how to spell.

➤ **Say the word.** Then close your eyes, and picture the way it's spelled. Spell it silently, and then write it.

➤ **Think of ways** to spell the vowel sound in a word. Try different spellings until the word looks right. For example, does *bild* look right or does *build* look right?

➤ **Think about the rules** that tell what spelling changes to make before adding -*ed* and -*ing* or changing *y* to *i*.

➤ **Think of a rhyming word** to help you figure out how to spell another word.

➤ **Make up a silly sentence** or phrase if it helps you remember how to spell a word. For example—

> If you can't remember how to spell *reign,* try a sentence such as *Ron's elegant iguana got nervous.* If you put together the first letters of each word, you have *reign!*

My own strategy . . .

Proofreading Strategies

➤ **Proofread your work twice.** The first time, circle words you know are misspelled. Then go back and look for words that you are not sure about.

➤ **Read the words backward.** Start with the last word and end with the first word. That may sound funny, but it may help you notice words that are misspelled!

➤ **Look for homophones,** and make sure each word you've written makes sense.

➤ **Make a chart to keep track of your spelling errors.** Then you can see what kinds of mistakes you make and work to correct them.

My own strategy . . .

How to Make Your Personal Word Log

A Personal Word Log is your own word collection. It's a place where you can store words that are special to you—words you need to know for classes, words with unusual meanings, or just words that you think are interesting. How can you develop your Personal Word Log? Here are some tips.

➤ **Watch for** especially interesting or unusual words when you're reading. Jot them down, and then add them to your Log!

➤ **When you watch** television or listen to the radio, listen for any new words that you would like to save. The word might be used by a favorite entertainer. Maybe it's a word used during a news broadcast.

➤ **Include words** that you need to use when you write, especially words that are hard for you to spell.

➤ **Include words** you have trouble spelling or pronouncing.

➤ **Think about** technical words used in your school subjects—mathematics, social studies, science.

➤ **Before you write** a word in your Log, check the spelling. You might look up the word in a dictionary or a thesaurus or ask a classmate for help.

➤ **Here's a helpful hint:** Keep notes on your words. To help you remember the meaning of a word, write a definition, a synonym, or an antonym. You might also use the word in a sentence. Or, write anything you remember about the word that makes it interesting. Look at the sample on the next page.

WORD AND NOTES

serendipitous

Serendipitous has a dip in the middle.

Serendipitous means "finding something by accident."

While flipping through a library book, she made a serendipitous discovery—a five-dollar bill.

Personal Word Log

You'll find your own Personal Word Log in the back of the book, starting on page 112.

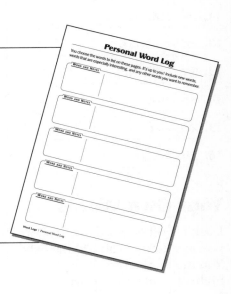

Lesson 1: Short Vowels

Spelling Words

1. sack
2. admit
3. rapid
4. glance
5. contact
6. contract
7. advance
8. depth
9. comment
10. summit
11. sketch
12. nonsense
13. splendid
14. ethnic
15. liquid
16. impulse

Your Own Words

Look for other words with short vowel sounds to add to the lists. You may notice an *exit* sign on a highway *ramp* to the airport. You might find *lodge* or *unpack* in a story about a vacation.

17. _____
18. _____
19. _____
20. _____

Each Spelling Word has one or two short vowel sounds. Look at the words to see how each short vowel sound is spelled.

Sort the Spelling Words into two groups. First, write the words that have one vowel sound. Then, write the words that have two vowel sounds.

ONE VOWEL SOUND
muff

_____   _____
_____   _____

TWO VOWEL SOUNDS
mitten

_____   _____
_____   _____
_____   _____
_____   _____
_____   _____
_____   _____

A short vowel sound is usually spelled with one vowel letter.

➤ **The letter *a* spells the short *a* sound in *pan*.**
➤ **The letter *e* spells the short *e* sound in *pet*.**
➤ **The letter *i* spells the short *i* sound in *pin*.**
➤ **The letter *o* spells the short *o* sound in *pot*.**
➤ **The letter *u* spells the short *u* sound in *pun*.**

Lesson 1: Short Vowels *(continued)*

SPELLING CLUES: Listening to Short Vowels   When you are unsure how to spell a word, say the word to yourself. Think about the short vowel sounds. Be sure you have used the correct vowel letter to spell each short vowel sound.

Say each word to yourself. Listen to the vowel sounds. Write the correct spelling of each word.

1. contract   contrect
2. comment   commint
3. liqued   liquid
4. nonsense   nonsinse
5. seck   sack
6. ethnic   ethnec

PROOFREADING   7–12. Proofread these road signs. Circle the misspelled words. Then write the words correctly.

7. One mile to the summet
8. Ahead—splended view
9. Unsafe for rapped driving
10. Call 555-0123 to contect road service
11. Flooded road—addvance with care
12. Soto Canyon—debth 2112 feet

FUN WITH WORDS   Write Spelling Words to replace 13–16.

I _13_ THAT I FEEL NERVOUS UP HERE.

I FEEL BRAVE ENOUGH TO LOOK OUT AT THE VIEW, THOUGH, AND EVEN TO _14_ DOWN TOWARD THE GROUND.

I'LL GET OUT A PENCIL AND _15_ THE VIEW.

WHY DIDN'T YOU TELL ME YOU FELT AN _16_ TO JUMP?

1. _____
2. _____
3. _____
4. _____
5. _____
6. _____
7. _____
8. _____
9. _____
10. _____
11. _____
12. _____

13. _____
14. _____
15. _____
16. _____

Lesson 2: Long Vowels

Spelling Words

1. bait
2. peach
3. bride
4. prime
5. globe
6. grove
7. slope
8. slice
9. roast
10. spike
11. stroke
12. praise
13. squeeze
14. breathe
15. gross
16. thigh

Your Own Words

Add other words with long vowel sounds to the lists. You might find *beach* and *whale* in an article about animal behavior. You might use *coast* and *tide* in a report about oceans.

17. _____
18. _____
19. _____
20. _____

Each Spelling Word has one long vowel sound. Look at the words to see how the long vowel sounds are spelled.

Say the Spelling Words to yourself, and sort them into four groups according to their vowel sounds.

kite
_____ _____
_____ _____
_____

sea
_____ _____
_____

lake
_____ _____

boat
_____ _____
_____ _____
_____

A long vowel sound is usually spelled with two or more letters in combination. In most combinations, the first vowel letter stands for the long vowel sound.

ELEMENTS OF LANGUAGE | Introductory Course | *Spelling*

Lesson 2: Long Vowels *(continued)*

SPELLING CLUES: Long Vowel Sounds When you write, think about the long vowel sounds in the words you are using. Be sure you have used the right combination of vowels to spell each long vowel sound.

Add a vowel or vowels to make a Spelling Word. Write the word.

1. gr__ss
2. th__gh
3. sp__k__
4. br__d__
5. r__ __st
6. gr __v__

PROOFREADING 7–12. Proofread these sentences. Circle the misspelled word in each sentence. Then write the word correctly.

- The perfect pech is large, ripe, juicy, just picked, and still warm from the sun.
- It's a mistake to squeese a fruit to see whether it is ripe.
- The rock broke loose and tumbled down the sloap.
- She signed the contract with a strook of her pen.
- How fast can you eat that sliece of watermelon?
- He won races for the fun of it, not for the prase and the prizes.

FUN WITH WORDS Write a word with a vowel sound for the first clue in each pair. Then add a letter to make a Spelling Word with a long vowel sound for the second clue. Write each Spelling Word you form on the right, too.

13. a mammal that flies   __ __ __
    something used to
    catch fish   __ __ __ __
14. very polite and proper   __ __ __ __
    most important   __ __ __ __ __
15. a slight movement
    of air   __ __ __ __ __ __
    to use the lungs   __ __ __ __ __ __ __
16. a rounded lump   __ __ __ __
    a sphere or ball   __ __ __ __

1. _____
2. _____
3. _____
4. _____
5. _____
6. _____
7. _____
8. _____
9. _____
10. _____
11. _____
12. _____
13. _____
14. _____
15. _____
16. _____

Lesson 3: Variant Vowels

Spelling Words

1. count
2. county
3. salt
4. cross
5. shout
6. youth
7. amount
8. pounds
9. mountain
10. thousands
11. proof
12. crawled
13. account
14. launched
15. rumors
16. saucer

Your Own Words

Look for other words with the /ou/, /ô/, or /o͞o/ sound, and add them to your lists. When might you use the words *astronaut* and *soundproof*? Where would you see the words *laundry* and *tools*?

17. _____
18. _____
19. _____
20. _____

Each Spelling Word has the /ou/ sound, the /ô/ sound, or the /o͞o/ sound. Study the words to see which letter or letter combinations are used to spell these sounds.

Say the Spelling Words to yourself, and sort them into three groups according to their vowel sounds.

/OU/
_____   _____
_____   _____
_____   _____
_____

/Ô/
_____   _____
_____   _____
_____

/O͞O/
_____   _____
_____

➤ **The /ou/ sound is often spelled *ou*.**

➤ **The /ô/ sound may be spelled *o, a, au,* or *aw*.**

➤ **The /o͞o/ sound may be spelled *ou, oo,* or *u*.**

Lesson 3: Variant Vowels *(continued)*

SPELLING CLUES: Reading Aloud When you are not certain of the correct spelling of a word, try to remember how the word looks. Then write the word down. Does it look right?

Check the two spellings of each pair. Write the correct spelling of each word.

1. yooth   youth   **4.** sault   salt

2. crauled   crawled   **5.** pounds   puonds

3. cross   crose   **6.** amount   amownt

PROOFREADING 7–12. Proofread this paragraph. Circle the misspelled words, and write the correct spelling of each.

> Libby and I sometimes watched an anthill up the street. One day she gave a showt for me to come and see. Tiny ants had lawnched an attack on the anthill. Big ants poured out by the thousands. Libby tried to cownt them and couldn't. There were too many to acount for. They fought a great battle on the hill—to them, it was a mountian. The big ants succeeded in driving their attackers away.

FUN WITH WORDS Write the Spelling Words to replace 13–16.

1. _____
2. _____
3. _____
4. _____
5. _____
6. _____

7. _____
8. _____
9. _____
10. _____
11. _____
12. _____

13. _____
14. _____
15. _____
16. _____

Lesson 4: Vowels Before *r*

Spelling Words

1. *roar*
2. *apart*
3. *reward*
4. *worse*
5. *turtle*
6. *nightmare*
7. *burnt*
8. *curb*
9. *purse*
10. *declare*
11. *scarce*
12. *inserts*
13. *sparkling*
14. *source*
15. *nervous*
16. *warrant*

Your Own Words

Look for other words that have a vowel before *r* to add to the lists. You might read about *Mars* and *Mercury* in a science article. You might see *stars* and *planetarium* at a science museum.

17. _____
18. _____
19. _____
20. _____

Each Spelling Word has a vowel sound followed by *r*: /är/, /âr/, /ûr/, or /ôr/. Look at the Spelling Words to see how these vowel sounds are spelled.

Say the Spelling Words to yourself, and sort them into four groups according to their vowel sounds.

/ÄR/
start
_____
_____
_____

/ÂR/
stare
_____
_____
_____

/ÛR/
lurch
_____
_____
_____
_____
_____
_____

/ÔR/
soar
_____
_____
_____
_____
_____

➤ **The /är/ sound is usually spelled *ar*.**

➤ **The /âr/ sound may be spelled *ar* or *are*.**

➤ **The /ûr/ sound may be spelled *ur, or,* or *er*.**

➤ **The /ôr/ sound may be spelled *oar, ar,* or *our*.**

Lesson 4: Vowels Before *r* *(continued)*

SPELLING CLUES: Comparing Spellings When you proofread, look for words that may be misspelled. If you rewrite the word in another way, you can often see which spelling is correct.

Look at the two possible spellings in each pair. Write the spelling that looks correct. Use the Spelling Dictionary if you need help.

1. aport   apart
2. insurts   inserts
3. scearce   scarce

4. purse   perse
5. declare   declair
6. cirb   curb

PROOFREADING 7–11. Proofread this phone message. Circle the misspelled words, and write the correct spelling of each.

> *Your sourse on the cargo plane story called. He says there was a small fire when the plane landed, but only part of the craft birnt. Both pilots say the damage could have been much wors. Now they're nervous, though, because they've heard there might be a warrent for their arrest. Also, your source wants to know if he will get a reword for the information he's providing.*

1. _____
2. _____
3. _____
4. _____
5. _____
6. _____

7. _____
8. _____
9. _____
10. _____
11. _____

FUN WITH WORDS Write Spelling Words to replace 12–16.

12. _____
13. _____
14. _____
15. _____
16. _____

Unit 1 Review
Practice Test: Part A

Read each sentence. On the answer sheet, fill in the letter of the correctly spelled word.

EXAMPLE: Climb the _____.
    A stairz   **B** sterz   **C** stairs   **D** sters

1. The train is _____.
    A rapud   **B** rapid   **C** rappid   **D** rappud

2. You can _____ the scene.
    A sketch   **B** skech   **C** scetch   **D** skeatch

3. I drank the _____.
    A likuid   **B** liqid   **C** liqued   **D** liquid

4. The _____ moves slowly.
    A tertle   **B** turtel   **C** tertul   **D** turtle

5. What _____ is the sea?
    A deepth   **B** defth   **C** depth   **D** deeph

6. The _____ is high.
    A montain   **B** mountain   **C** mounten   **D** mowtane

7. Do you _____ a ham?
    A roast   **B** roste   **C** rost   **D** roest

8. Tom hurt his _____.
    A thiegh   **B** thyh   **C** thigh   **D** thy

9. You need _____ to fish.
    A bate   **B** baite   **C** bayt   **D** bait

10. Please _____ the bread.
    A slise   **B** slyce   **C** slais   **D** slice

EXAMPLE
(A) (B) (C) (D)

ANSWERS
1 (A) (B) (C) (D)
2 (A) (B) (C) (D)
3 (A) (B) (C) (D)
4 (A) (B) (C) (D)
5 (A) (B) (C) (D)
6 (A) (B) (C) (D)
7 (A) (B) (C) (D)
8 (A) (B) (C) (D)
9 (A) (B) (C) (D)
10 (A) (B) (C) (D)

Unit 1 Review *(continued)*
Practice Test: Part B

Read each group of phrases. Find the underlined word that is misspelled. On the answer sheet, fill in the letter for that word.

EXAMPLE:

  A good <u>manners</u>   **C** simple <u>question</u>

  B bad <u>habbits</u>   **D** <u>tricky</u> puzzle

1. **A** <u>acount</u> of a story   **C** <u>cross</u> the road
   B <u>launched</u> a rocket **D** a playful <u>youth</u>

2. **A** <u>breathe</u> freely   **C** <u>bride</u> and groom
   B <u>prime</u> time   **D** <u>squeaze</u> a lemon

3. **A** offer <u>proof</u>   **C** a worm <u>crawled</u>
   B several <u>pounds</u>   **D** heard <u>roumers</u>

4. **A** around the <u>globe</u>   **C** count a <u>gross</u>
   B gave <u>praize</u>   **D** hammer a <u>spike</u>

5. **A** torn <u>apart</u>   **C** very <u>nervus</u>
   B <u>burnt</u> down   **D** <u>sparkling</u> water

6. **A** eat a <u>peach</u>   **C** on an <u>impulse</u>
   B scream and <u>showt</u> **D** <u>contact</u> a friend

7. **A** <u>glance</u> quickly   **C** <u>declair</u> loudly
   B pay a <u>reward</u>   **D** <u>scarce</u> supply

8. **A** leather <u>purse</u>   **C** add <u>salt</u>
   B the news <u>source</u>   **D** a lot of <u>nonsense</u>

9. **A** make a <u>coment</u>   **C** at the <u>summit</u>
   B <u>ethnic</u> group   **D** <u>splendid</u> party

10. **A** <u>roor</u> loudly   **C** in the <u>county</u>
   B orange <u>grove</u>   **D** advance <u>slowly</u>

EXAMPLE

Ⓐ   Ⓑ   Ⓒ   Ⓓ

ANSWERS

1   Ⓐ   Ⓑ   Ⓒ   Ⓓ

2   Ⓐ   Ⓑ   Ⓒ   Ⓓ

3   Ⓐ   Ⓑ   Ⓒ   Ⓓ

4   Ⓐ   Ⓑ   Ⓒ   Ⓓ

5   Ⓐ   Ⓑ   Ⓒ   Ⓓ

6   Ⓐ   Ⓑ   Ⓒ   Ⓓ

7   Ⓐ   Ⓑ   Ⓒ   Ⓓ

8   Ⓐ   Ⓑ   Ⓒ   Ⓓ

9   Ⓐ   Ⓑ   Ⓒ   Ⓓ

10   Ⓐ   Ⓑ   Ⓒ   Ⓓ

Unit 1 Review *(continued)*
Activities

What's in a Word?

ET

The word *ET* is actually an abbreviation of the less familiar word *extraterrestrial*. The two parts of this word make its meaning clear. The prefix *extra-* means "outside" or "beyond." The base word *terrestrial* means "one who inhabits the earth." So an extraterrestrial is a being that lives somewhere beyond earth.

grasshopper/cricket

The *grasshopper* is a well-named insect. It usually lives in and eats grass, and it has an amazing ability to hop or leap. Grasshoppers use their legs to make chirping sounds.

Very closely related to the *grasshopper* is the *cricket*, which also makes chirping sounds. For centuries, crickets have been considered lucky animals. People in China, Japan, and other Asian countries have kept crickets as "singing" pets.

Imaginative Words

Combine parts of two Spelling Words with each other to form made-up words—for example, *contract* and *nonsense* might be combined to form *consense*. Make up your own words, based on at least six of your Spelling Words. Show the words to a group of classmates. Have them identify the Spelling Words in each made-up word.

Partner Spelling

Write clues for five Spelling Words. Then switch clues with a partner. Write the Spelling Words that match your partner's clues. Then change papers again and check each other's answers.

Picture Clues

Do this activity with a partner. Each partner should draw simple characters or scenes as clues to three Spelling Words. Trade drawings with your partner. Identify and write the correct Spelling Word under each of your partner's clues.

Proofreading Partners

Do this activity with a partner. Each of you should make a list of five Spelling Words that give you trouble or that you think are the most challenging to spell. Exchange lists. Each partner then writes a paragraph in which the other person's five words are misspelled. Then exchange papers, and proofread and correct each other's paragraphs. Be sure each Spelling Word is spelled correctly.

Unit 1 Review (continued)
Activities

Spelling Partners

Make flashcards for five Spelling Words you find challenging. Work with a partner who has also made five flashcards. Turn all ten cards face down on a desk. Take turns choosing a card, reading the word, and asking for the correct spelling. If the word is spelled correctly, the speller keeps the card. Otherwise, the card is returned, face down, to the desk.

WHAT IS IN A WORD?

Start your own collection of word histories. Trace the development of at least two words from each lesson. Keep your collection in a separate notebook. Add to it not just Spelling Words but new and interesting words you come across in your reading.

ENDURANCE SPELLING

With a partner, play a game to review the Spelling Words. Read the words, and ask your partner to spell each word aloud as quickly as possible. Then switch roles. Which of you can *endure* the pressure and spell all the words correctly?

What's in a Word?

phantom
Phantom can be another word for *imaginary*. Alice, for example, wandered through Wonderland, a place that seemed real to her but was completely imaginary.

prejudice
A *prejudice* is an unfair opinion that is formed before one knows all the relevant facts. The word begins with the prefix *pre-*, which means "before." Recalling the meaning of this prefix and thinking of the base word *judge* can help you remember that a prejudice is a judgment made before it should be—made without all the facts.

Lesson 6: Other Vowel Spellings

Spelling Words

1. busy
2. among
3. building
4. young
5. enough
6. though
7. straight
8. rough
9. courage
10. eighth
11. system
12. although
13. sleigh
14. boulder
15. biscuit
16. dough

Your Own Words

Look for other words with unusual vowel spellings to add to your lists. Where might you see the words *businesses* and *freight*? A health article might tell you that a *shoulder* injury is *tough* to heal.

17. _____
18. _____
19. _____
20. _____

These Spelling Words have unusual spellings of certain vowel sounds. Study the words to see how the short *i* sound, the short *u* sound, the long *a* sound, and the long *o* sound are spelled.

Say the Spelling Words to yourself, and sort them into four groups, each representing a different vowel sound. Three example words are given. Fill in the last one as you are sorting.

gym
____
____
____
____

tongue
____
____
____
____

weigh
____
____
____
____

____
____
____
____

➤ In some words, the short *i* sound is spelled *u*, *ui*, *y*, or *a*.
➤ The short *u* sound is sometimes spelled *ou* or *o*.
➤ In some words, the long *a* sound is spelled *aigh* or *eigh*.
➤ The long *o* sound is sometimes spelled *ough* or *ou*.

ELEMENTS OF LANGUAGE | Introductory Course | *Spelling*

Lesson 6: Other Vowel Spellings *(continued)*

SPELLING CLUES: Word Shapes Sometimes, thinking about the shape of a word can help you remember the correct spelling. Is the whole word long and flat? Does a letter at the beginning of the word drop below the line, or do two letters at the end rise above the others?

Write the Spelling Word that fits each shape.

1. ▭

4. ▭

2. ▭

5. ▭

3. ▭

6. ▭

PROOFREADING 7–10. Proofread these paragraphs. Circle the misspelled words, and write each word correctly.

"Did you have a ruff day posing for photographers?" Dana's sister asked her.

Dana laughed and shook her head. Her sister went on, "Well, if you're not too bissy signing autographs, you can help me get dinner ready. Why don't you start by mixing this douh? Althogh Mom and Dad will probably want one bisket each, you and I can eat two!"

WORKING WITH MEANING Study the picture. The two questions below the picture have words missing. Write the Spelling Word that best fits each blank.

There is one tree __12__ the __13__s.
Would you have __14__ __15__ to try climbing that __16__ wall?

1. _____
2. _____
3. _____
4. _____
5. _____
6. _____

7. _____
8. _____
9. _____
10. _____
11. _____
12. _____
13. _____
14. _____
15. _____
16. _____

Lesson 7: Words with *ie* and *ei*

Spelling Words

1. boyfriend
2. girlfriend
3. mischief
4. pier
5. freight
6. foreign
7. receive
8. receiver
9. belief
10. relief
11. weighed
12. reins
13. fierce
14. heights
15. thieves
16. achieve

Your Own Words

Notice other words with the vowel combinations *ie* and *ei*, and add those words to the lists. You might find *chief* or *sleigh* in a story about a winter rescue. When might you use *shield* or *reign*?

17. _____
18. _____
19. _____
20. _____

Each Spelling Word includes the vowel combination *ei* or *ie*. Study the words in the list to see what sounds each vowel combination can spell.

Sort the Spelling Words into two groups, one with the vowel combination *ei* and one with the vowel combination *ie*.

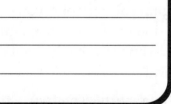

ie	ei
_____	_____
_____	_____
_____	_____
_____	_____
_____	_____
_____	_____
_____	_____
_____	_____

➤ **The long *e* sound, the short *e* sound, and the short *i* sound are sometimes spelled by the letters *ie*.**

➤ **The long *a* sound, the long *e* sound, the short *i* sound, and the long *i* sound are sometimes spelled by the letters *ei*.**

Lesson 7: Words with *ie* and *ei* (continued)

SPELLING CLUES: Letter Patterns When you are learning a word with an unusual spelling, say the word aloud and study the pattern of the letters. Then visualize the spelling. See the letter pattern in your mind.

Look at each pair of words, and think about the correct letter pattern. Write the correct spelling.

1. acheive   achieve
2. receive   recieve
3. releif   relief
4. reseaver   receiver
5. foriegn   foreign

1. _____
2. _____
3. _____
4. _____
5. _____

PROOFREADING 6–12. Proofread this paragraph. Circle the misspelled words, and write those words correctly.

What Is a Hero?

Does a hero leap from great hights or capture feirce lions? Does a hero chase dangerous theives until they fall off the end of a peir into the icy ocean? Does a hero grab the riens of a runaway stallion or stop a frieght train when the tracks have been washed out? Or could a hero be just a neighbor with a strong beleif in himself or herself and a willingness to help others?

6. _____
7. _____
8. _____
9. _____
10. _____
11. _____
12. _____

FUN WITH WORDS Write the Spelling Words that answer these questions.

13. Which Spelling Word does the adjective *mischievous* come from?
14. Which Spelling Word rhymes with *neighed?*
15–16. Which two Spelling Words name a close pal?

13. _____
14. _____
15. _____
16. _____

Lesson 8: Compound Words

Spelling Words

1. greenhouse
2. seashore
3. fireworks
4. fun-loving
5. New Year
6. fairy tales
7. bedtime
8. cupboard
9. upright
10. teenager
11. thunderstorm
12. barefoot
13. mean-spirited
14. middle-aged
15. bodyguard
16. so-called

Your Own Words

Add to the lists other compound words you find in your reading and writing. You might see *fun house* or *merry-go-round* at a carnival. When might you write *football* or *touchdown*?

17. _____
18. _____
19. _____
20. _____

Each Spelling Word is a compound word. Look at each one, and see what two smaller words make up the compound.

Sort the Spelling Words in a way that will help you remember them.

sea   horse
_____   _____
_____   _____

sea - lane
_____ - _____
_____ - _____
_____ - _____
_____ - _____

seagoing
_____   _____
_____   _____
_____   _____
_____   _____
_____   _____

A compound word is made up of two or more shorter words. The spelling of these shorter words remains the same. Most compound words are written as one word. Some are written as two words, and others are hyphenated.

Lesson 8: Compound Words *(continued)*

SPELLING CLUES: Checking Compound Words When you proofread your own writing, be sure each smaller word within a compound word is spelled correctly.

Check each pair of words. Write the correct spelling.

1. bodyguard   bodygaurd
2. uprite   upright
3. Newyear   New Year
4. thunderstrom   thunderstorm
5. mean-spiritid   mean-spirited
6. so-called   socalled

1. _____
2. _____
3. _____
4. _____
5. _____
6. _____

PROOFREADING 7–12. Proofread this journal entry. Circle each misspelled word, and then write the word correctly.

> When these so-called hard times are over, I'm going to be a funloving teeager. I'll go to the seeshore with my friends. We'll stay up long past our bed-time—after all, we're not midle-age. We'll watch fire works exploding in the sky, and we'll feel safe and happy because life has returned to normal!

7. _____
8. _____
9. _____
10. _____
11. _____
12. _____

FUN WITH WORDS Write the Spelling Word that fits each clue.

13. Nearly all animals—including bears—walk this way.
14. These stories end happily and fairly.
15. It doesn't have to be made of wood, and you can keep much more than cups inside.
16. It isn't green, and no people actually live there.

13. _____
14. _____
15. _____
16. _____

Lesson 9: Homophones

Spelling Words

1. week
2. weak
3. steel
4. steal
5. grown
6. groan
7. guest
8. guessed
9. creek
10. creak
11. weather
12. whether
13. sore
14. soar
15. stake
16. steak

Your Own Words

Look for other homophones to add to the lists. You might read *cord* (which has the homophone *chord*) in a book about knots. When might you use the word *isle* or *aisle*?

17. _____
18. _____
19. _____
20. _____

Each Spelling Word has a homophone, another word that has the same pronunciation but a different meaning and a different spelling. Look at the words, and notice how the homophones in each pair are spelled.

Sort the Spelling Words into two lists, with one half of a pair of homophones in each list.

ONE SYLLABLE
cord   **chord**

_____   _____
_____   _____
_____   _____
_____   _____
_____   _____
_____   _____

TWO SYLLABLES
affect   **effect**

_____   _____

Homophones are pairs of words that sound the same but have different spellings and different meanings.

NAME _____   CLASS _____   DATE _____

Lesson 9: Homophones *(continued)*

SPELLING CLUES: Spelling and Meaning When you learn to spell a word that has a homophone, learn the spelling and meaning of both words. As you use the two words, keep their meanings in mind.

Write the Spelling Word that fits each brief definition.

1. To take what doesn't belong to you—*steel* or *steal?*
2. A strong metal—*steel* or *steal?*
3. A slice of meat or fish—*stake* or *steak?*
4. A stick sharpened at one end—*stake* or *steak?*

PROOFREADING 5–10. Circle each incorrect homophone and write the correct word.

- Have you guest how many olives are on that pizza?
- If your estimate is correct, you'll win an extra-large pizza every weak, for a whole year!
- If I won, I'd be so excited I'd feel week in the knees.
- Would you invite a guessed to share your pizza?
- Would you eat the pizza by yourself until you were so full you had to grown?
- Do you think that you'll have groan tired of pizza by the end of the year?

WORKING WITH MEANING Each sentence is missing a pair of homophones. Write the Spelling Words that complete each sentence.

I wonder __11__ the __12__ is going to change.
I don't really want to __13__ today, because my throat is so __14__.
I think I hear my hang glider __15__ every time I go over this __16__.

1. _____
2. _____
3. _____
4. _____
5. _____
6. _____
7. _____
8. _____
9. _____
10. _____

11. _____
12. _____
13. _____
14. _____
15. _____
16. _____

Lesson 10: Easily Confused Words

Spelling Words

1. later
2. latter
3. except
4. accept
5. angle
6. angel
7. costume
8. custom
9. affect
10. effect
11. adopt
12. adapt
13. device
14. devise
15. decent
16. descent

Your Own Words

Look for other pairs of words to add to the lists. You might read *prosecute*—easily confused with *persecute*—in a news story. Where might you find *desert* printed in place of *dessert*?

17. _____
18. _____
19. _____
20. _____

Words that sound similar and have similar spellings can be easily confused. Each Spelling Word is similar to another Spelling Word. However, each word in the pair has its own pronunciation, meaning, and spelling. Study the Spelling Words, and think about the differences between the two words in each pair.

Sort the Spelling Words into two groups according to which syllable is accented.

ACCENT ON FIRST SYLLABLE

_____   _____
_____   _____
_____   _____
_____

ACCENT ON SECOND SYLLABLE

_____   _____
_____   _____
_____   _____
_____   _____
_____

Words with similar spellings can be easily confused. To determine the correct spelling, listen to the word and think about how it is used.

ELEMENTS OF LANGUAGE | Introductory Course | *Spelling*

Lesson 10: Easily Confused Words *(continued)*

SPELLING CLUES: Using Definitions When choosing between two similar words, think about what each word means. Use the spelling that matches the meaning you want.

Write the Spelling Word that fits each brief definition.

1. to figure out
2. the second of two
3. to influence
4. going down
5. an instrument
6. a sharp turn

1. _____
2. _____
3. _____
4. _____
5. _____
6. _____

PROOFREADING 7–12. Proofread this article. Circle the misspelled words, and then write each word correctly.

Hogs Judged at Fair

It's the costume to award a blue ribbon to the biggest, most beautiful hog at the county fair. This year, two animals and their owners stepped up to except the ribbon. One animal was a decent champion hog, but the other was a dog in custom. The dog's entrance had a noticeable affect on the crowd. Everyone accept a few disappointed hog owners found the outfit very amusing. The dog's owners latter apologized to anyone who had been offended by their joke.

7. _____
8. _____
9. _____
10. _____
11. _____
12. _____

WORKING WITH WORDS Write Spelling Words to replace 13–16.

13. _____
14. _____
15. _____
16. _____

Unit 2 Review
Practice Test: Part A

Read each sentence. On the answer sheet, mark the answer to indicate whether the spelling of the underlined word is correct or incorrect.

EXAMPLE: Can you play the <u>peano</u>?
correct   incorrect

1. I had a <u>bisquit</u> for breakfast.
correct   incorrect

2. Roll the <u>dough</u> until it's soft.
correct   incorrect

3. You have <u>grone</u> tall.
correct   incorrect

4. Follow that <u>straigh</u> path.
correct   incorrect

5. That lion has a <u>fierce</u> look.
correct   incorrect

6. Which puppy did you <u>addopt</u>?
correct   incorrect

7. The <u>frieght</u> train stopped.
correct   incorrect

8. It's <u>bed-time</u> now.
correct   incorrect

9. I have two <u>middleaged</u> aunts.
correct   incorrect

10. The doors always <u>creak</u>.
correct   incorrect

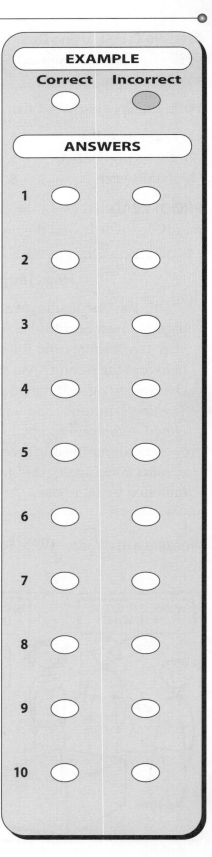

EXAMPLE — Correct / Incorrect

ANSWERS 1–10

Unit 2 Review (continued)
Practice Test: Part B

On the answer sheet, mark the letter of the correctly spelled word that makes sense in the sentence.

EXAMPLE: Don't _____ food.
A waist   B waste   C wayst   D wast

1. Kay _____ the answer.
A guest   B gest   C guessed   D gessed

2. The bridge is _____.
A steel   B steal   C steele   D stele

3. I feel _____ and dizzy.
A weak   B weke   C week   D weake

4. The _____ approached.
A thunder-storm   C thundarstorm
B thundorstorm   D thunderstorm

5. You have much _____!
A curage   B courege   C courage   D carrage

6. I'll visit you _____.
A latter   B later   C layter   D laiter

7. The law will _____ you.
A affect   B effect   C afect   D efect

8. Two lines form an _____.
A angel   B angle   C anjile   D anjel

9. I'd like a _____ job.
A descent   B desent   C decent   D dessent

10. They did _____ a gift.
A recieve   B reseeve   C receave   D receive

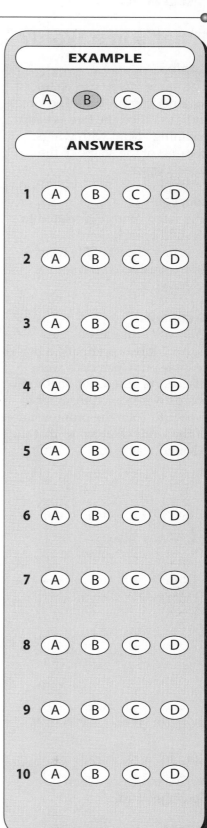

EXAMPLE
A B C D

ANSWERS
1 A B C D
2 A B C D
3 A B C D
4 A B C D
5 A B C D
6 A B C D
7 A B C D
8 A B C D
9 A B C D
10 A B C D

Unit 2 Review (continued)
Activities

What's in a Word?

catalpa
The name *catalpa* can be traced to American Indians. The Creek Indians called the tree *kutuhlpa*, meaning "head with wings," because of the shape of the tree's flowers.

courage
The word *courage* is related to the Old French word *cuer*, meaning "heart." The heart is often considered the source of courage.

◆ cupboard
Cupboard is literally a "cup board." It was originally a board or table on which cups were placed. As time went on, the two words were joined together as *cupboard*. Then the pronunciation of the word changed so that the *p* sound was lost.

Checking Up
Work with three or four classmates. Together, look up in a dictionary the Spelling Words from one of the lessons in this unit. Discuss the meanings given for each word. Make a note of some of the meanings that you haven't thought about before.

Synonym Spell-Check
Work with a partner to review some of your Spelling Words. Think of synonyms for four Spelling Words. Give your partner each synonym in turn, and ask him or her to identify and then spell the Spelling Word.

Proofreading Partners
Do this activity with a partner. Each of you should make a list of five Spelling Words that give you trouble or that you consider the most challenging in the unit. Exchange lists. Write a paragraph using your partner's five Spelling Words, but misspelling them. Then exchange papers, and proofread and correct each other's paragraphs. Be sure each Spelling Word is spelled correctly.

◆ This indicates a Unit Spelling Word.

Unit 2 Review (continued)
Activities

Tongue Twisters

Write a short tongue twister that includes at least three Spelling Words. Have a classmate check your spelling before he or she attempts to say the tongue twister faster.

Homophone Fun

Think of a sentence in which you can use a pair of homophones that are Spelling Words. Write the sentence, but leave blanks for the homophones. Challenge a classmate to fill in the blanks with the correct Spelling Words.

Secret Messages

Do this activity with a partner. Each of you should write a secret message using abbreviations. Exchange secret messages, and figure out what word each abbreviation stands for. Write the words. Then exchange papers again, and check that the correct word has been used in place of each abbreviation.

Antonym Spelling

Work with a partner to review at least five Spelling Words. Give your partner an antonym of a Spelling Word as a clue. Then ask your partner to guess and spell the word.

What's in a Word?

giraffe
From the fourteenth to the sixteenth centuries, the *giraffe* was called the camelopard. This name comes from the Greek word *kamelopardalis.* The ancient Greeks believed that the *giraffe* was part camel because of its height and part leopard because of its spots.

heroine
The word *heroine* comes from the Greek word *heros,* which means "a person of great courage." In the legends of ancient Greece, a hero was a person who had more courage and strength than ordinary people—though not as much as the gods. Incredibly strong Hercules, for example, was a hero in the ancient Greek myths.

spectator
A *spectator* is a person who watches without participating. The word *spectator* comes from the Latin verb *spectare,* which means "to look at." The main characters in many books and stories are spectators who observe the activities of other people.

Lesson 12: Changing *y* to *i*

Spelling Words

1. cities
2. mummies
3. supplies
4. families
5. varied
6. centuries
7. colonies
8. applies
9. occupied
10. identified
11. enemies
12. activities
13. denied
14. allied
15. industries
16. qualified

Your Own Words

Look for other words to add to the lists. You might read an article about museums and note *studied* or *discoveries*. In writing about the articles, you might use *duties* or *worried*.

17. _____
18. _____
19. _____
20. _____

Each Spelling Word comes from a base word that ends with a consonant followed by *y*. Look at the words, and notice the ending that was added to each base word. Think about how the spelling was changed by that addition.

Sort the Spelling Words into two lists, according to their endings. One example word is given. Fill in the other one as you are sorting.

countries

_____   _____
_____   _____
_____   _____
_____   _____

_____   _____
_____   _____
_____   _____

If a word ends in a consonant and *y*, change the *y* to an *i* before adding *-es* or *-ed*.

Lesson 12: Changing *y* to *i* (continued)

SPELLING CLUES: Spelling Rules Think about the rule that applies to adding an ending to base words that end in a consonant and *y*. Follow the rule when you add *-es* or *-ed* to these words.

Add the ending in parentheses to the base word. Write the word.

1. supply (-es)
2. enemy (-es)
3. ally (-ed)
4. industry (-es)
5. colony (-es)
6. apply (-es)

PROOFREADING 7–12. Proofread this note. Circle the misspelled words, and write the words correctly.

> We're having a great trip! Our guide keeps us ocupied with interesting activitys and fascinating tours. We've seen jewelry that is centureys old, fabulous statues, and paintings decorated with gold. What I like best, of course, is seeing real mummys!
>
> There are four other famlies on the tour, so I have plenty of kids to spend time with. We've been to five citys so far—one more and we'll be on our way home.

WORKING WITH MEANING Write Spelling Words to replace 13–16.

1. _____
2. _____
3. _____
4. _____
5. _____
6. _____
7. _____
8. _____
9. _____
10. _____
11. _____
12. _____
13. _____
14. _____
15. _____
16. _____

Lesson 13: Unstressed Endings /ər/, /əl/, /ən/

Spelling Words

1. reader
2. speaker
3. layer
4. American
5. beaten
6. musical
7. rotten
8. German
9. Indian
10. Roman
11. explorer
12. stretcher
13. critical
14. criminal
15. political
16. original

Your Own Words

As you read and write, look for other words that end with the sounds /ər/, /əl/, and /ən/, and add them to the lists. You may read *comical* or *writer* in a biography. When might you use the word *Mexican* or *financial?*

17. _____
18. _____
19. _____
20. _____

Each Spelling Word ends with the sounds /ər/, /əl/, or /ən/. These sounds always occur in an unaccented syllable of a word.

Sort the Spelling Words into three lists, according to the sound of their endings.

teacher

_____   _____

_____   _____

_____

theatrical

_____   _____

_____   _____

_____

African

_____   _____

_____   _____

_____

The sounds /ər/, /əl/, or /ən/ occur in an unaccented syllable, usually at the end of a word. The sound /ər/ is usually spelled *er*. The sound /əl/ is often spelled *al*. The sound /ən/ is usually spelled *an* or *en*.

Lesson 13: Unstressed Endings /ər/, /əl/, /ən/
(continued)

SPELLING CLUES: Best-Guess Spelling Sometimes when you write, you may not want to stop to check the spelling of a word. If you are unsure of a spelling, write the word, using your best guess, and make a check mark above the word. Later, you can verify the spelling of the words you have marked.

Write these best-guess words correctly.

1. Americun
2. pollitical
3. reder

4. Germun
5. crimnal
6. exsplorer

PROOFREADING 7–12. Proofread this note. Circle the misspelled words, and write each word correctly.

> What rotton luck! My orignal idea was to help our baseball team avoid being beatin. I raced back to catch a criticle fly ball. Unfortunately, I fell before I reached the ball. I put out my arm—and what a pain! I was carried off the field on a strecher. The next thing I knew, a doctor was putting the final laier of plaster on my wrist cast.

WORKING WITH MEANING Write Spelling Words for 13–16.

a ___13___ soldier

an ___14___ weaver

a public ___15___

a ___16___ instrument

1. _____
2. _____
3. _____
4. _____
5. _____
6. _____
7. _____
8. _____
9. _____
10. _____
11. _____
12. _____
13. _____
14. _____
15. _____
16. _____

Lesson 14: Spelling Patterns—VC/CV Words

Spelling Words

1. pillow
2. indeed
3. monster
4. fifteen
5. escape
6. gotten
7. velvet
8. engine
9. insist
10. admire
11. index
12. intense
13. further
14. frantic
15. convince
16. instinct

Your Own Words

Look for other words to add to the lists. You might see *commute* or *trolley* on city signs. You might write *dolphin* or *hornet* in a science report.

17. _____
18. _____
19. _____
20. _____

Each Spelling Word has two syllables, with a consonant at the end of the first syllable and another consonant or group of consonants at the beginning of the second syllable. Study the list, and think about the pattern of vowel-consonant-consonant-vowel (VC/CV) in this group of Spelling Words.

Sort the Spelling Words into three groups, according to the consonant groups in the middle of the words.

DOUBLE CONSONANT
ar/row
_____
_____

TWO DIFFERENT CONSONANTS
hel/met
_____
_____
_____
_____
_____
_____
_____
_____
_____
_____

CONSONANT PLUS CLUSTER OR DIGRAPH
ab/stain
_____
_____
_____

Many two syllable words follow the vowel-consonant-consonant-vowel (VC/CV) pattern. In these words, the first syllable usually has a short vowel sound.

ELEMENTS OF LANGUAGE | Introductory Course | *Spelling*

Lesson 14: Spelling Patterns—VC/CV Words
(continued)

SPELLING CLUES: Syllabication When you come to the end of a line, you sometimes have to divide a word into syllables. A word that has the VC/CV pattern may be divided between the middle consonants.

Divide these words into syllables, using a hyphen.

1. further   **3.** fifteen   **5.** indeed

2. engine   **4.** instinct   **6.** gotten

PROOFREADING 7–13. Proofread the paragraph. Circle the misspelled words and write each word correctly.

How Would You Treat a Princess?

If a princess from another century appeared in your living room, would you slip a velvit pilow under her feet? Or would you ensist that she addmire your favorite TV show? Would you urge her to tell stories about the brave knight who captured a threatening monstor? Or would you try to convience her that modern times are the best? How would you feel if she simply wanted to excape?

FUN WITH WORDS Write Spelling Words for 14–16.

14. If you get very nervous flying above water, you may feel __14__ over the Atlantic.

15. If you're afraid of what might happen to the hero of a movie, you'll experience __15__ suspense.

16. If you're always checking the reference section at the back of a book, you may have an __16__ reflex.

1. _____

2. _____

3. _____

4. _____

5. _____

6. _____

7. _____

8. _____

9. _____

10. _____

11. _____

12. _____

13. _____

14. _____

15. _____

16. _____

Lesson 15: Spelling Patterns—V/CV Words

Spelling Words

1. Friday
2. apron
3. motive
4. meter
5. agent
6. evil
7. local
8. eager
9. famous
10. fiber
11. razor
12. vital
13. rival
14. basis
15. cheetah
16. scenic

Your Own Words

Look for other two-syllable V/CV words to add to the lists. You might notice *depot* and *hotel* in an article about a frontier town. When might you write the words *motion* and *vocal*?

17. _____
18. _____
19. _____
20. _____

In each of these two-syllable Spelling Words, the first syllable ends with a vowel and the second syllable begins with a consonant (V/CV). Look at the words, and think about the vowel sounds in each. The first syllable of each word has a long vowel sound.

Sort the Spelling Words into four groups according to the vowel sound in the first syllable of each word. Three examples are given. Fill in the last one as you are sorting.

ra/dar
_____
_____
_____
_____
_____

pre/fix
_____
_____
_____
_____
_____

si/lent
_____
_____
_____
_____

_____
_____
_____

A two-syllable word may contain the V/CV pattern. In these words, the first syllable usually has a long vowel sound.

Lesson 15: Spelling Patterns—V/CV Words *(continued)*

SPELLING CLUES: Proofreading Syllables When you are unsure of the spelling of a word with more than one syllable, check the word one syllable at a time. Be sure you have used a letter or letter combination to spell each sound.

Check the two spellings in each pair. Write the correct spelling of each word.

1. eager   eagre   **3.** Friday   Friady
2. bassis   basis   **4.** rivle   rival

PROOFREADING 5–12. Proofread the paragraph. Circle each misspelled word, and write its correct spelling.

    Imagine living in this old castle! If you're interested, you can ask the real estate agant to take you on a tour. She'll point out the seenic setting, the beautiful gardens, the many fireplaces, and the stone walls, a metter thick. The animal park even has a tame cheeta. Of course, she may not mention the vitel fact that you can't use a toaster and an electric raisor at the same time. She is also unlikely to tell you that for centuries the locol people have been telling stories of evvil deeds that took place here.

FUN WITH WORDS Write Spelling Words to replace 13–16.

1. _____
2. _____
3. _____
4. _____

5. _____
6. _____
7. _____
8. _____
9. _____
10. _____
11. _____
12. _____

13. _____
14. _____
15. _____
16. _____

Unit 3 | Lesson 15

33

Lesson 16: Adding -*ed* and -*ing*

Spelling Words

1. lifted
2. cooling
3. pointed
4. returned
5. speaking
6. spelling
7. wondered
8. bragged
9. healed
10. scrubbed
11. answered
12. threatened
13. admitted
14. committed
15. referring
16. preferred

Your Own Words

Look for other words with the -*ed* and -*ing* endings, and add them to the lists. You might see *concurring* and *acquitted* in a story about a trial. You might use *dreamed* and *telling* in a journal entry.

17. _____
18. _____
19. _____
20. _____

Each Spelling Word ends with -*ed* and -*ing*. Notice that in some cases the addition of the ending changes the spelling of the base word.

Sort the Spelling Words into two groups to help you remember them. Two example words are given.

ADD -ED AND -ING
played

_____   _____
_____   _____
_____   _____
_____   _____
_____   _____

DOUBLE THE CONSONANT AND ADD -ED AND -ING
rubbed

_____   _____
_____   _____
_____   _____

The endings -*ed* and -*ing* can be added to many words without changing the spelling of the base word. If a word ends with one vowel followed by one consonant, usually the final consonant is doubled if

➤ it is a one-syllable word
➤ it is a two-syllable word and the accent is on the second syllable

Lesson 16: Adding *-ed* and *-ing* (continued)

SPELLING CLUES: Spelling Rules Think about the rules for adding -ed and -ing to a base word. Follow the rule that applies to each word.

Add the ending in parentheses to the base word. Write the word.

1. threaten (ed) **3.** scrub (ed) **5.** refer (ing)

2. lift (ed) **4.** cool (ing) **6.** admit (ed)

PROOFREADING 7–10. Proofread this notice. Circle the misspelled words. Then write each word correctly.

Needed: Host Family

Do you believe that problems between countries can be healled by increasing understanding?
Is your family commited to helping others?
Are you willing to share your home, to answer
pointted questions, and to offer someone help
in speaking English? If so, you may be ready
to host one of our foreign exchange students.
Applications from families with teenagers are prefered.

WORKING WITH MEANING Write Spelling Words for 11–16.

Have you ever heard someone __11__ like this?

Haven't you __14__ if this happens when the papers are __15__?

1. _____

2. _____

3. _____

4. _____

5. _____

6. _____

7. _____

8. _____

9. _____

10. _____

11. _____

12. _____

13. _____

14. _____

15. _____

16. _____

THAT __12__ TEST WAS TOO EASY!

THAT MATH QUIZ WAS NO PROBLEM! I __13__ EVERY QUESTION CORRECTLY.

OH NO! IF ONLY I HADN'T __16__!

Unit 3 Review
Practice Test: Part A

Read the four possible spellings for each word. On the answer sheet, mark the letter of the correct spelling.

EXAMPLE:
- A robbot
- B robat
- C robot
- D robott

1. A aprin
   B apron
   C aprun
   D aperon

2. A supplies
   B supplys
   C suplies
   D suplys

3. A familes
   B famillies
   C fammilies
   D families

4. A ocuppied
   B ocupied
   C occupied
   D ocupyed

5. A threatened
   B theatned
   C thretened
   D threatend

6. A Indiun
   B Indian
   C Indeen
   D Indien

7. A speakar
   B speakir
   C speeker
   D speaker

8. A musicle
   B musiccal
   C musical
   D muzical

9. A ingine
   B engene
   C enjine
   D engine

10. A pilloe
    B pillo
    C pillow
    D pillowe

EXAMPLE

A B (C) D

ANSWERS

1 A B C D
2 A B C D
3 A B C D
4 A B C D
5 A B C D
6 A B C D
7 A B C D
8 A B C D
9 A B C D
10 A B C D

Unit 3 Review (continued)
Practice Test: Part B

Read each phrase. On the answer sheet, mark the letter of the correctly spelled word.

EXAMPLE: remember _____
    A cleerly   **B** clearly   **C** clirly   **D** clerly

1. discuss _____
    A furthar   **B** farthar   **C** furthur   **D** further

2. _____ route
    A senic   **B** cenic   **C** scenic   **D** scenick

3. _____ completely
    A convinse   **B** convince   **C** convins   **D** convinsce

4. _____ to memory
    A comitted   **C** committed
    B commited   **D** comited

5. _____ night
    A Friday   **B** Fridy   **C** Fridey   **D** Fryday

6. the _____ painting
    A original   **B** orginal   **C** orignal   **D** originall

7. _____ the charge
    A denyed   **B** dinied   **C** deanied   **D** denied

8. _____ one to another
    A prefered   **B** preferred   **C** preffered   **D** prefferred

9. _____ person
    A faimous   **B** famise   **C** famous   **D** famuse

10. _____ off
    A coling   **B** coleing   **C** cooling   **D** coolling

EXAMPLE
(A) (B) (C) (D)

ANSWERS
1 (A) (B) (C) (D)
2 (A) (B) (C) (D)
3 (A) (B) (C) (D)
4 (A) (B) (C) (D)
5 (A) (B) (C) (D)
6 (A) (B) (C) (D)
7 (A) (B) (C) (D)
8 (A) (B) (C) (D)
9 (A) (B) (C) (D)
10 (A) (B) (C) (D)

Unit 3 Review *(continued)*
Activities

What's in a Word?

castle
The English word *castle* developed from the Latin word *castellum*, meaning "small fort." Today, *castle* may mean either "a large fortified building or set of buildings" or "a large, elegant house."

◆ *escape*
Escape is a word that people sometimes spell incorrectly. They say or write it as if the word were "excape" instead of the correct form, *escape*. This is probably because the prefix *ex-* is often used to mean "out from a place." The word *escape* has the same meaning. *Ex-* words of this type include *exit, expel, extract, extend,* and *export.*

meditation
The word *meditation* is a noun formed from the verb *meditate* and the suffix *-ion*. *Meditate* means "to think quietly and deeply over a period of time."

Partner Spelling
Write clues for five Spelling Words. Then switch clues with a partner. Write the Spelling Words that match your partner's clues. Then change papers again and check each other's answers.

Spelling Cards
With a group of classmates, make a set of sixteen cards, each with the base word form of a Spelling Word. Then take turns drawing a card and challenging other group members to spell the base word and the Spelling Word with its ending, either *-ed* or *-ing*.

Say It Quickly
Play this game in a group. The goal is speed. Going clockwise, players take turns naming number prefixes or combining forms, such as *demi-, pent-, hex-, hept-, cent-, kilo-*. As soon as a player names a prefix or a combining form, anyone can call out a word that begins with the prefix or combining form. The first person to say a word beginning with that prefix or combining form gets a point, and the person who called out the prefix or combining form writes the word down. Then the next person in the circle calls out a prefix or a combining form, and the game continues. The player with the most points wins.

◆ This indicates a Unit Spelling Word.

Unit 3 Review *(continued)*
Activities

Pick a Card, Any Card

Work with a small group, and write each of the Spelling Words in this unit on a separate index card. Then place the cards face down on a table, mix them up, and take turns picking one. The person who picks the card says the word, spells it, and then uses it in a sentence.

A FINAL SCRAMBLE

Choose three Spelling Words and scramble the letters in each. Challenge a partner to unscramble the letters and spell each word correctly.

Proofreading Partners

Do this activity with a partner. Each of you should make a list of five Spelling Words that give you trouble or that you think are the most difficult to spell correctly. Exchange lists. Each partner should write a paragraph in which the other person's five words are misspelled. Then exchange papers, and proofread and correct each other's paragraphs. Be sure each Spelling Word is spelled correctly.

What's in a Word?

mesmerize
The word *mesmerize* comes from a person, Franz Anton Mesmer. Mesmer was a physician, and he developed the treatment now known as hypnosis.

museum
You might go to a museum to see an exhibit of ancient Egyptian mummies. The word *museum* comes from an ancient Greek word meaning "the place of the Muses." Greek mythology told of nine sisters who were goddesses of arts and sciences. These nine sisters were known as the Muses.

phobia
A *phobia* is "a strong and persistent fear." *Claustrophobia*, for example, is "fear of being closed in."

Lesson 18: Noun Suffix *-ance/-ence*

Spelling Words

1. importance
2. entrance
3. difference
4. independence
5. insurance
6. conference
7. ambulance
8. absence
9. instance
10. audience
11. allowance
12. intelligence
13. assurance
14. appearance
15. obedience
16. presence

Your Own Words

Add other words with the suffixes *-ance* and *-ence* to the lists. You might notice the word *distance* or *circumference* in a math problem. Where might you see the word *performance* or *fragrance?*

17. _____
18. _____
19. _____
20. _____

Each Spelling Word ends with *-ance* or *-ence.* The suffix *-ance* or *-ence* can be added to many words or roots to form nouns.

Study each Spelling Word and note the suffix. Then sort the words into two groups according to the suffix.

-ANCE fragrance	-ENCE excellence
_____	_____
_____	_____
_____	_____
_____	_____
_____	_____
_____	_____
_____	_____

The suffixes *-ance* and *-ence* mean "quality of" or "state of." Words ending in these suffixes are usually nouns.

There is no rule that governs whether a word ends with *-ance* or *-ence.* Use a dictionary whenever you are not sure which spelling is correct.

Lesson 18: Noun Suffix *-ance/-ence* (continued)

SPELLING CLUES: Words with Suffixes When you write, notice words that end with *-ance* or *-ence*. Make sure you have spelled the suffix correctly. Use a dictionary if you are unsure of the correct spelling.

Proofread these words. Write the word if it is spelled correctly. If the word is misspelled, write it correctly.

1. presence
2. insurence
3. conferance

4. assurance
5. allowence
6. importence

PROOFREADING 7–12. Proofread this advertisement. Circle the words that are misspelled. Then write each word correctly.

> Do you think your dog has too much independance to be trained? Are you afraid it lacks the intellegence to learn simple commands? Just give the dog to us! You'll notice a huge differance after only ten hours of training in obediance. For instence, your dog will walk at your side, will come when you call, and will not misbehave in your presence or even in your absense!"

FUN WITH WORDS Write Spelling Words to complete items 13–16.

1. _____
2. _____
3. _____
4. _____
5. _____
6. _____
7. _____
8. _____
9. _____
10. _____
11. _____
12. _____
13. _____
14. _____
15. _____
16. _____

I'LL BOW AND SMILE TO THE JUDGES WHEN I MAKE MY 13 . THEY LIKE A DOG TO HAVE A FRIENDLY 14 .

DID I TELL YOU WHAT HAPPENED AT THE LAST DOG SHOW? I PLAYED DEAD FOR SO LONG THE JUDGES HAD TO CALL AN 15 ! THE 16 LOVED IT!

21st DOG AWARDS

Lesson 19: Noun Suffixes -*ship*, -*ment*, -*ity*

Spelling Words

1. statement
2. friendship
3. leadership
4. partnership
5. activity
6. ability
7. argument
8. personality
9. electricity
10. championship
11. community
12. majority
13. responsibility
14. curiosity
15. necessity
16. authority

Your Own Words

Look for other words with the suffixes -*ship*, -*ment*, and -*ity* to add to the list. You might hear *hardship* or *tournament* in a sportscast. You might see *creativity* or *appointment* on a report card.

17. _____
18. _____
19. _____
20. _____

Each Spelling Word has the suffix -*ship*, -*ment*, or -*ity*. These suffixes can be added to many words to form nouns.

Look at each word. Notice whether the spelling of the base word changes or stays the same when the suffix is added. Then sort into groups by suffix.

-SHIP
_____
_____
_____
_____

-ITY
_____
_____
_____
_____
_____
_____
_____
_____

-MENT
_____
_____

The suffixes -*ship*, -*ment*, and -*ity* can be added to words to form nouns.

➤ **Most words retain their spelling when -*ship* or -*ment* is added.**

➤ **When -*ity* is added to a word that ends in *e*, the *e* is dropped.**

Lesson 19: Noun Suffixes -*ship*, -*ment*, -*ity* (continued)

SPELLING CLUES: Suffixes If you're not sure how to spell a word, look at its parts. Make sure the suffix is spelled correctly. Then look at the base word and decide whether the spelling stays the same or changes.

Look at the two possible spellings. Write the correct spelling.

1. statement   statment
2. athorrity   authority
3. majorrity   majority
4. partneship   partnership
5. electricity   electrisity
6. argument   arguement

PROOFREADING 7–12. Proofread this notice. Circle the words that are misspelled, and write them correctly.

> This dog has never won a champeonship, but if you're looking for friendshep, he's a real winner. His strong sense of curiousity sometimes gets him into trouble, but he has the abbility to know when his master has had enough! He would thrive in a house filled with acttivity. Because of his size, a house with a large yard in a rural community is a nessesity.

WORKING WITH MEANING Use Spelling Words to replace 13–16.

1. _____
2. _____
3. _____
4. _____
5. _____
6. _____
7. _____
8. _____
9. _____
10. _____
11. _____
12. _____

13. _____
14. _____
15. _____
16. _____

Lesson 20: Prefix *ad-* (*ac-, as-, af-, ap-*)

Spelling Words

1. appointed
2. accident
3. affair
4. assembly
5. approach
6. accuse
7. applause
8. affection
9. accompany
10. assign
11. appreciate
12. accurate
13. association
14. apparent
15. accustomed
16. assistance

Your Own Words

Add other words with the prefix *ad-* (*ac-, as-, af-,* or *ap-*).

17. _____
18. _____
19. _____
20. _____

The prefix *ad-* may also be spelled *ac-, as-, af-,* or *ap-*. Each Spelling Word begins with one spelling of this prefix. Note the double consonant in each word.

Sort the words into groups according to the spelling of the prefix.

AC-
_____
_____
_____
_____

AF-
_____
_____

AP-
_____
_____
_____

AS-
_____
_____
_____

The prefix *ad-* (*ac-, as-, af-,* and *ap-*) can be added to many Latin roots to form nouns and verbs. A double consonant occurs where the prefix joins the root word.

The prefix *ad-* is spelled

➤ *ac-* when added to roots beginning with *c*
➤ *as-* when added to roots beginning with *s*
➤ *af-* when added to roots beginning with *f*
➤ *ap-* when added to roots beginning with *p*

Lesson 20: Prefix *ad- (ac-, as-, af-, ap-)* (continued)

SPELLING CLUES: Words With Prefixes When you proofread your work, check for words that begin with *ac-, as-, af-,* or *ap-.* If these are prefixes, the consonant is usually doubled. Then check the rest of the word for correct spelling.

Proofread these words. Write the word if it is spelled correctly. If the word is misspelled, write it correctly.

1. axcident
2. aplause
3. approch
4. assocation

5. asembly
6. acustomed
7. assitance
8. appreciate

PROOFREADING 9–12. Proofread the following letter. Circle the words that are misspelled. Then write each word correctly.

> Dear Jen,
> Here's the picture you asked for. By the way, the dog near the fence is Misty. My neighbors have apointed me her baby sitter while they're away. I don't like to acuse anyone, even a dog, of being crazy, but it's apparent that Misty is very strange. The dog stares at me for hours! Now that you have an acurate picture of me, do you think it's because of the way I look, or do you think it's her way of showing afection?

FUN WITH WORDS Write the Spelling Word that belongs in each blank. The underlined word is a clue.

13. Did you go to the <u>carnival</u> yesterday?
    No, I couldn't. What kind of _____ was it?
14. Could you _____ me to the store and help me do the shopping? We're having <u>guests</u> for dinner.
15. I wonder if Mr. Hixson will _____ a lot of homework.
    No way! Didn't you see the <u>notice</u> that school will be closed tomorrow?
16. Lisa had no idea that her <u>father</u> would come to the costume party dressed as a giant raisin. Her shock was _____ to everyone.

1. _____
2. _____
3. _____
4. _____
5. _____
6. _____
7. _____
8. _____

9. _____
10. _____
11. _____
12. _____

13. _____
14. _____
15. _____
16. _____

Lesson 21: Prefix *com-* *(con-)*

Spelling Words

1. conviction
2. commanded
3. commonly
4. considered
5. continued
6. commander
7. commit
8. constitution
9. confusing
10. commence
11. commotion
12. commercial
13. communicate
14. communities
15. communication
16. committee

Your Own Words

Look for other words that begin with *com-* and *con-* to add to the lists. You might see *communism* or *commonwealth* in a social studies book. You might use *conform* or *conduct* in an essay about behavior.

17. _____
18. _____
19. _____
20. _____

Each Spelling Word begins with *com-* or *con-*, which means "together" or "with." Note the doubling of the consonant in many of the words.

Sort the words into groups by whether the consonant is doubled.

WITH DOUBLE CONSONANT
commune

_____   _____
_____   _____
_____   _____
_____   _____
_____

WITHOUT DOUBLE CONSONANT
constant

_____   _____
_____   _____
_____

Com- and con- are prefixes that mean "together" or "with." Words that begin with com- have a double m if the prefix is joined to a root word that begins with m.

Lesson 21: Prefix: *com- (con-)* *(continued)*

SPELLING CLUES: Prefixes When you write, watch for words that begin with *com-* or *con-*. Be sure you have used a double consonant if the base word or root begins with *m* or *n*.

Determine which prefix, *com-* or *con-*, belongs with each of these word parts. Then write the word correctly.

1. _____stitution   4. _____monly
2. _____mander   5. _____mence
3. _____munities   6. _____mercial

PROOFREADING 7–11. Proofread this dialogue. Circle the words that are incorrectly spelled, and write them correctly.

Joshua: You should have connitnued talking to her. Why did you tell her you had to leave?

Michael: Well, there was all this comotion around her. A whole group of people—it looked like a commity—was asking her something.

Joshua: What makes you think she's not ready to comit herself to helping us? Have you considerd the fact that this is in her interest too?

WORKING WITH MEANING Write Spelling Words to replace 12–16.

1. _____
2. _____
3. _____
4. _____
5. _____
6. _____
7. _____
8. _____
9. _____
10. _____
11. _____
12. _____
13. _____
14. _____
15. _____
16. _____

Lesson 22: Unstressed Ending *-ant/-ent*

Spelling Words

1. absent
2. important
3. current
4. president
5. elephant
6. confident
7. instant
8. element
9. servant
10. excellent
11. opponent
12. permanent
13. assistant
14. innocent
15. significant
16. sufficient

Your Own Words

Look for other words ending in *-ant* or *-ent* to add to the lists. You might use *elegant* or *magnificent* to describe a place. Where might you find the words *immigrant* and *descendant*?

17. _____
18. _____
19. _____
20. _____

Unstressed vowels often occur in word endings such as *-ant* and *-ent*. These two word endings sound alike. Study the Spelling Words to see how each word ends.

Sort the words into two groups. Use the word endings as a guide.

-ANT

_____ _____
_____ _____
_____ _____

-ENT

_____ _____
_____ _____
_____ _____
_____ _____

There is no rule that tells whether *-ant* or *-ent* is correct.

Knowing the spelling of another form of the word is often helpful.

➤ **Examples: *instance/instant, absence/absent***

Lesson 22: Unstressed Ending *-ant/-ent* (continued)

SPELLING CLUES: Mnemonics A *mnemonic* device is a trick or strategy to help you remember something. You might, for example, remember that *immigrant* ends in *-ant* by making up a sentence such as "The immigrant came to this country." The *a* in *came* will remind you that *immigrant* ends in *-ant*.

Write the correctly spelled word in each pair. Then make up a sentence or a phrase to help you remember the spelling of any three of the words.

1. elephent   elephant
2. apsent   absent
3. presedent   president
4. permanent   permanant
5. servant   servent
6. opponant   opponent

1. _____
2. _____
3. _____
4. _____
5. _____
6. _____

PROOFREADING 7–12. Proofread the following newspaper headlines. Circle the misspelled word in each, and write it correctly.

Recorder — Curent Strategy for Research Undergoes Important Change **7.**

GAZETTE — Scientists Announce Signifigant Progress in Fossil Identification **8.**

Star News — Missing Elemant in Formula for X-Ray Vision Discovered **9.**

TRIBUNE — Laboratory Assisstant Accused of Causing Explosion **10.**

SENTINEL — Police Confedent That Laboratory Mystery Will Be Solved **11.**

Journal News — Vaccine to Prevent Shyness an Instent Success **12.**

7. _____
8. _____
9. _____
10. _____
11. _____
12. _____

FUN WITH WORDS Complete this limerick by writing the missing Spelling Words.

The scientist looked very __13__.
His background looked better than __14__.
His job was __15__,
But he did what he oughtn't,
Once again, looks just were not __16__.

13. _____
14. _____
15. _____
16. _____

Unit 4 Review
Practice Test: Part A

Read the four possible spellings for each word. On the answer sheet, mark the letter of the correct spelling.

EXAMPLE:

A camputer C computer
B camputar D computar

1. A inteligence C intelligense
   B intelligence D inteligense

2. A neccessity C necessity
   B neccesity D necesity

3. A absence C abscense
   B abscence D absense

4. A aplausse C applauze
   B applause D applouse

5. A electricity C ellectricity
   B elictricity D electricty

6. A assistance C asistence
   B assistence D asistance

7. A excellant C excellent
   B excelent D eksellent

8. A communitys C communittes
   B comunities D communities

9. A ledership C liedership
   B leedership D leadership

10. A appriciate C appreciate
    B appreceate D apreciate

EXAMPLE

Ⓐ Ⓑ Ⓒ Ⓓ

ANSWERS

1 Ⓐ Ⓑ Ⓒ Ⓓ

2 Ⓐ Ⓑ Ⓒ Ⓓ

3 Ⓐ Ⓑ Ⓒ Ⓓ

4 Ⓐ Ⓑ Ⓒ Ⓓ

5 Ⓐ Ⓑ Ⓒ Ⓓ

6 Ⓐ Ⓑ Ⓒ Ⓓ

7 Ⓐ Ⓑ Ⓒ Ⓓ

8 Ⓐ Ⓑ Ⓒ Ⓓ

9 Ⓐ Ⓑ Ⓒ Ⓓ

10 Ⓐ Ⓑ Ⓒ Ⓓ

Unit 4 Review *(continued)*
Practice Test: Part B

One word in each sentence is misspelled. On the answer sheet, mark the letter of the underlined word that is misspelled.

EXAMPLE: Please <u>riturn</u> the <u>atlas</u>.
            A   B

1. The <u>commitee</u> <u>continued</u> its discussion.
       A   B

2. A <u>commercial</u> should never be <u>confussing</u>.
       A   B

3. The <u>statment</u> left no room for <u>argument</u>.
       A   B

4. The <u>asistant</u> arrived in an <u>instant</u>.
       A   B

5. His <u>servant</u> rode on an <u>elephent</u>.
       A   B

6. Having <u>sufficent</u> food is <u>important</u>.
          A   B

7. The <u>ambulance</u> used the front <u>entrence</u>.
       A   B

8. The new <u>partnership</u> has aroused much <u>curiocity</u>.
            A   B

9. The <u>assembily</u> of a bike is a complicated <u>affair</u>.
       A   B

10. The <u>presense</u> of a large <u>audience</u> is important.
        A   B

EXAMPLE	
(A)	B

ANSWERS	
1	A	B
2	A	B
3	A	B
4	A	B
5	A	B
6	A	B
7	A	B
8	A	B
9	A	B
10	A	B

Unit 4 Review *(continued)*
Activities

What's in a Word?

◆ *ambulance*

Ambulance comes from the Latin word for "walk." At first an ambulance was a "walking hospital." Medical personnel moved along with an army in the field so that they could give aid to wounded soldiers as quickly as possible.

◆ *commercial*

The word *commercial* means "having to do with business." TV and radio *commercials* get their name because they are trying to get more business for a company.

◆ *constitution*

The word *constitution* can literally mean "what something is made of." It could be said that the *Constitution* of the United States is what this country is made of. The *Constitution* describes the basic system and workings of our government and serves as the highest law of the land.

◆ *innocent*

The word *innocent* means "not having committed a crime." Many people think that a jury finds someone *innocent* of a crime, but that is not true. The person is found *not guilty* of the crime, which is not the same thing. The verdict of *not guilty* means that the prosecutor did not prove that the person was guilty. The person does not have to prove he or she is *innocent;* the prosecutor has to prove that he or she is *guilty.*

◆ This indicates a Unit Spelling Word.

Challenge Yourself

Choose five Spelling Words that you find difficult. When you have chosen your five words, write a sentence using each of them. Leave a blank where the Spelling Word belongs. Then, without looking at the Spelling Words, fill in the blanks, trying to spell the words correctly. When you are finished, check your spelling.

SUFFIX SCRAMBLE

Work with a partner. Write the Spelling Words in this unit on cards. Take turns choosing a card. Give each other a clue about the word on the card you have chosen. For example, if you choose the word *majority,* you could say, "This word describes a group and ends in -*ity*." Each correct answer is worth one point.

Prefixes That Describe Where

English uses many prefixes that describe where. *De-* means "from" or "down." To *decay* is "to fall *from* goodness or soundness; to rot." To *deport* is "to send *from* a place." *Ex-* means "out." To *explode* is "to burst *outward*." All the prefixes in the list describe where.

a-	=	on	*mid-*	=	middle
ab-	=	from	*para-*	=	beside
by-	=	near, aside	*peri-*	=	around
circum-	=	through, across	*retro-*	=	back
epi-	=	upon	*sub-*	=	under
extra-	=	outside	*super-*	=	over
hypo-	=	under	*tele-*	=	distant
im- (in-)	=	into	*trans-*	=	across
intra-	=	within			

Work with a partner to see how many words you can come up with, using each prefix from the list. Compare your list with that of another pair of students. Combine your lists, and add up the total.

Unit 4 Review (continued)
Activities

Spelling Check-Up

Choose five Spelling Words that give you difficulty. Write a sentence using each word, but leave a blank where the Spelling Word belongs. Then, without looking at your list of Spelling Words, complete the sentence by filling in the correct word. Check your spelling after you have finished.

Fantastic Folks

Play this game with a group of four. Divide the Spelling Words by the number of people in the group so that each person has four Spelling Words. Each person should create a fictitious person's name and habits, beginning with each assigned Spelling Word. Try to include alliteration and rhyme (the sillier the better). For example, *Curiosity kept Carol creeping through the crypt.* Share your sayings with your group. Then choose three favorites, write them down, and add them to a class collection.

Proofreading Partners

Do this activity with a partner. Each of you should make a list of five Spelling Words that give you trouble or the five words you consider the most challenging in general. Exchange lists. Each partner should write a paragraph on any topic you choose. Use your partner's five Spelling Words in your paragraph, but misspell them. Then exchange papers, and proofread and correct each other's paragraphs. Be sure each Spelling Word is spelled correctly.

What's in a Word?

laid-back
Laid-back usually describes a relaxed, easygoing person.

psychology
Psychology comes from the Greek word for *mind—psyche*—plus the suffix *-ology,* which means "the study of." People interested in psychology try to understand the reasons behind people's behavior. To create believable characters, writers need insight into human psychology.

raza
Raza, which is Spanish for the English word *race,* can mean a group of people sharing a common tradition, language, or culture.

triumph
The word *triumph* has a long history. Years ago, Roman generals who defeated their enemies in battle made a grand entrance into Rome, proud of their victory and the riches they had won. The Latin word for such a victorious entrance was *triumphus.* Today, conquering a fear, winning a race, or making a friend can all be considered triumphs.

transmutation
Before the era of modern science, some people believed that ordinary metals could be changed into precious metals. People who believed in such a change, or *transmutation,* practiced a combination of science and magic.

Lesson 24: Spelling Patterns—More VCV Words

Spelling Words

1. prison
2. linen
3. palace
4. climate
5. talent
6. novel
7. treason
8. comic
9. profit
10. token
11. weapon
12. gopher
13. pleasant
14. siren
15. frigid
16. spiral

Your Own Words

Find your own VCV words, and add them to the lists. For example, you might read about the *damage* to a *motel* in an article about a fire. When might you use the words *pilot* and *placid*?

17. _____
18. _____
19. _____
20. _____

Each Spelling Word has a vowel-consonant-vowel combination. Think about the vowel sound in the first syllable in each word.

Sort the Spelling Words according to whether the vowel sound in the first syllable is long or short.

titan

finish

Some words have a VCV pattern.

➤ If the pattern of the word is V/CV, the vowel sound in the first syllable is usually long.

➤ If the pattern of the word is VC/V, the vowel sound in the first syllable is usually short.

Lesson 24: Spelling Patterns—More VCV Words
(continued)

SPELLING CLUES: Classifying Errors When you proofread, keep track of your spelling errors. Notice what kinds of mistakes you usually make, and work to correct them.

Check the two spellings in each pair. Write the correct spelling.

1. gopher   gophar
2. siron   siren
3. spirel   spiral
4. token   tokin
5. treason   treasen
6. linen   linin

PROOFREADING 7–12. Proofread this paragraph. Circle the spelling errors. Write the correct spelling.

    Heather had a talint for both writing and drawing so she decided to write a commic book. She made the evildoers end up in preson, in spite of their secret wepon, while the crime fighters not only won, they turned a profet and bought a palice.

WORKING WITH MEANING Write Spelling Words to replace 13–16.

1. _____
2. _____
3. _____
4. _____
5. _____
6. _____
7. _____
8. _____
9. _____
10. _____
11. _____
12. _____
13. _____
14. _____
15. _____
16. _____

IT'S A LITTLE __14__ FOR ME.

I THOUGHT WE WERE GOING SOUTH, TO MORE __15__ WEATHER.

WHAT DO YOU THINK OF THE __13__ IN THIS PART OF THE WORLD?

IT'S A __16__ EXPERIENCE. WE'RE ENJOYING THE CHANGE.

Lesson 25: Mixed Spelling Patterns

Spelling Words

1. banner
2. platform
3. hotel
4. funnel
5. habit
6. display
7. clever
8. gather
9. empty
10. chaos
11. suspense
12. Saturn
13. oval
14. orphan
15. fatal
16. crystal

Your Own Words

Look for words that follow these patterns to add to the lists. If you read a story about marine research, you might come across the words *bottom* and *sonar*. Where might you see *tribune* or *trial?*

17. _____
18. _____
19. _____
20. _____

Each Spelling Word has its own syllable pattern. Look at each word. Notice where the syllable breaks are in relation to the vowel and consonant sounds.

Sort the Spelling Words according to the vowel and consonant pattern of sounds in each word. Remember that a consonant sound may be formed by more than one letter. An example word for each list is given.

per/form (VC/CV)
_____
_____
_____
_____
_____
_____

mo/ment (V/CV)
_____
_____
_____

lav/ish (VC/V)
_____
_____
_____

dis/close (VC/CCV)
_____

fu/el (V/V)
_____

camp/site (VCC/CV)
_____

A word may be divided into syllables according to the pattern of vowel and consonant sounds. The consonant sound in these patterns may be formed by more than one letter.

Lesson 25: Mixed Spelling Patterns (continued)

SPELLING CLUES: Writing Aloud When you are having trouble writing a word, try saying the word aloud. Listen to the sounds in the word, and think about the letters that usually spell those sounds.

Read these spelling pairs aloud. Write the correct spelling for each word.

1. orphan   orfan
2. hottel   hotel
3. habbit   habit

4. choas   chaos
5. funnel   funel
6. fatal   fattal

PROOFREADING 7–12. Proofread this report. Circle the misspelled words, and write the correct spellings.

PRESIDENTIAL NEWS CONFERENCE

The President held a press conference in the Ovel Office today. On his desk was a desplay of the Argo, an underwater exploring device. On a plateform nearby was a model of a new device. A baner was suspended over it. "This cleaver new device will help us explore the planet Satturn," he said.

WORKING WITH MEANING Write Spelling Words to replace 13–16.

THE _13_ IS BROKEN, BUT THE SILVERWARE IS IN ONE PIECE.

THIS PART OF THE SHIP IS _14_. HAS SOMEONE ALREADY TAKEN THE TREASURE?

WE COULD _15_ THESE OLD COINS IN A FISHING NET TO TAKE THEM TO THE SURFACE.

I'M IN _16_. HOW MUCH WILL THESE BE WORTH?

1. _____
2. _____
3. _____
4. _____
5. _____
6. _____

7. _____
8. _____
9. _____
10. _____
11. _____
12. _____

13. _____
14. _____
15. _____
16. _____

Lesson 26: Unusual Plurals

Spelling Words

1. goldfish
2. trout
3. moose
4. cactus
5. media
6. fungi
7. bacteria
8. stimulus
9. stimuli
10. larvae
11. radius
12. nucleus
13. nuclei
14. species
15. salmon
16. hippopotamus

Your Own Words

Look for other words that have unusual plurals, and add them to the lists. In an aquarium, you might see the words *algae* and *jellyfish*. When might you use the words *curricula* and *alumni?*

17. _____
18. _____
19. _____
20. _____

Each Spelling Word is either an unusual plural or the singular form of an unusual plural.

Sort the Spelling Words in a way that will help you remember them. Three examples are given. Fill in the last one as you are sorting.

SINGULARS ENDING IN -US
octopus
_____
_____
_____
_____
_____

PLURALS ENDING IN -A OR -AE
data, alumnae
_____
_____
_____
_____
_____

OTHER
_____
_____
_____
_____
_____

PLURALS ENDING IN -I
alumni
_____
_____
_____
_____

Some words have unusual plural forms.

➤ **The plural form of words whose singular ends in -us often ends in -i.**

➤ **Some words have the same singular and plural form.**

➤ **Other unusual plural forms end in -a or -ae.**

ELEMENTS OF LANGUAGE | Introductory Course | *Spelling*

Lesson 26: Unusual Plurals (continued)

SPELLING CLUES: Word Shapes Sometimes thinking about the shape of a word can help you remember the correct spelling. Is the whole word long and flat? Does a letter at the beginning of the word drop below the line? Do two letters at the end rise above the others? Keep these shape clues in mind when you write.

Write the Spelling Word that fits each shape.

1. [shape box]

2. [shape box]

3. [shape box]

4. [shape box]

1. _____
2. _____
3. _____
4. _____

PROOFREADING 5-10. Proofread this paragraph. Circle the misspelled words and write each one correctly.

Jody had always been interested in goaldfishes, but the stimulius to take deep-sea diving lessons was a show he saw on public television. The medea reported that a scientist had found evidence that deadly bactera and funji had been invading the coral reefs. This was the reason that so many species were now endangered. Jody thought he might be able to help if he learned to dive but found he was not comfortable unless he stayed within a hundred-foot radias of the boat.

5. _____
6. _____
7. _____
8. _____
9. _____
10. _____

FUN WITH WORDS Read the rhymes, and write the Spelling Word that tells who or what is talking.

11. I'm a fish who has a very hard task.
    I swim upstream. Do you think I'll last?
12–13. One of me ends in *us*. An *i* ends two of me.
    To atoms we're a must. But we're very hard to see.
14. We started out as tiny eggs.
    We'll soon be bugs with
    many legs.
15. I live by the river.
    I'm too fat to dance.
    I drink lots of water and
    eat lots of plants.
16. I don't need much water.
    I don't like the sea.
    I do like the desert.
    Can you name me?

11. _____
12. _____
13. _____
14. _____
15. _____
16. _____

Unit 5 | Lesson 26

59

Lesson 27: Adjective Suffixes *-ive, -ous*

Spelling Words

1. *positive*
2. *attractive*
3. *effective*
4. *various*
5. *curious*
6. *tremendous*
7. *enormous*
8. *obvious*
9. *delicious*
10. *mysterious*
11. *executive*
12. *creative*
13. *fabulous*
14. *legislative*
15. *negative*
16. *sensitive*

Your Own Words

Look for other words that end in *-ive* or *-ous*, and add them to the lists. You may notice *gorgeous* in a story describing spring flowers. You might find *active* and *passive* in a story about animal behavior.

17. _____
18. _____
19. _____
20. _____

Each Spelling Word has a suffix that makes the word an adjective. Look at the words to see how they are spelled.

Sort the Spelling Words into two groups, according to their endings.

massive
_____   _____
_____   _____
_____   _____
_____   _____

infamous
_____   _____
_____   _____
_____   _____
_____   _____

The suffixes *-ive* and *-ous* are adjective-forming suffixes.

➤ **If the base word ends with *e*, drop the final *e* before adding *-ive* or *-ous*.**

➤ **If the base word ends with a consonant and *y*, change the *y* to *i* before adding *-ous*.**

Lesson 27: Adjective Suffixes *-ive, -ous* (continued)

SPELLING CLUES: Find the Base Word When a word is formed by adding a suffix to a base word, look at the base word. Think about the rules for adding a suffix when the base word ends with an *e* or a *y*.

Check the two spellings in each pair. Write the correct spelling of each word.

1. misterious
   mysterious

2. various
   varyous

3. legislative
   legeslative

4. efective
   effective

5. atracttive
   attractive

6. createive
   creative

PROOFREADING 7–12. Proofread these sentences about sea animals. Circle the misspelled word in each sentence, and then write the word correctly.

- Some fabulious sea animals are actually mammals.
- Many fish are sensative to light.
- Plankton makes a delicous meal for some sea animals.
- Whales can cause termendous water turbulence.
- An octopus, with its eight tentacles, is a courious-looking marine animal.
- Some people believe that sharks are an enormus menace to surfers.

WORKING WITH MEANING Write Spelling Words to replace 13–16.

1. _____
2. _____
3. _____
4. _____
5. _____
6. _____

7. _____
8. _____
9. _____
10. _____
11. _____
12. _____

13. _____
14. _____
15. _____
16. _____

Lesson 28: Words with Prefixes and Suffixes

Spelling Words

1. unlikely
2. repayment
3. reaction
4. replacement
5. unpredictable
6. disagreement
7. renewal
8. unemployment
9. unexpectedly
10. unfortunately
11. unusually
12. reproduction
13. reconstruction
14. disagreeable
15. unsuccessful
16. uncomfortable

Your Own Words

Look for other words with these prefixes and suffixes to add to the lists. Your parents might say that a *reinforcement* of rules is necessary if your room is in an *unhealthful* and *disorderly* state.

17. _____
18. _____
19. _____
20. _____

Each Spelling Word has a prefix and a suffix added to a base word. Notice that the spelling of these base words does not change when the prefix and suffix are added.

Sort the words into three groups based on their prefixes.

UN-
unknowable

RE-
reestablishment

DIS-
displacement

The prefixes *un-*, *re-*, and *dis-* change the meaning of a word but do not cause the spelling of the base word to change.

The suffixes *-able*, *-ment*, *-ly*, *-al*, *-ful*, and *-ion* change the way a word is used and sometimes cause the spelling of the base word to change.

Lesson 28: Words with Prefixes and Suffixes
(continued)

SPELLING CLUES: Prefixes and Suffixes When a word has both a prefix and a suffix, think about how the base word is spelled. Then ask yourself if the prefix or suffix might cause that spelling to change.

Add the prefix and suffix in parentheses to each base word. Write the word.

1. success (un-, -ful)   **4.** act (re-, -ion)
2. usual (un-, -ly)   **5.** pay (re-, -ment)
3. new (re-, -al)   **6.** construct (re-, -ion)

PROOFREADING 7–12. Proofread this note. Circle the six misspelled words. Then write the words correctly.

> Dear Linda,
> It is unexpectedly beautiful here! Unfortunetely, the picture I'm sending is a poor reproducksion of the scenery. Even though the weather is unpredictible, I am having an unusualy good time. I want to stay longer, but that's unlikly. I wouldn't want to face unnemployment when I get back!
>
>   See you soon,
>   Cody

WORKING WITH MEANING Use Spelling Words to replace 13–16.

1. _____
2. _____
3. _____
4. _____
5. _____
6. _____
7. _____
8. _____
9. _____
10. _____
11. _____
12. _____
13. _____
14. _____
15. _____
16. _____

ME, TOO. THE WEATHER IS WARM AND I'M 14 .

FRANKLY, I'M LOOKING FOR A 16 .

I'M IN A VERY 13 MOOD TODAY.

I HAD A 15 WITH A FRIEND THIS MORNING.

Unit 5 Review
Practice Test: Part A

Read the groups of four words. Find the underlined word that is spelled incorrectly. On the answer sheet, mark the letter for that word.

EXAMPLE:

A Spanish guitar

B paper clip

C weather report

D medicel test

1. A interesting novel
   B king's palice
   C loads of linen
   D frigid weather

2. A huge hippopotamus
   B tasty samon
   C creative arts
   D obvious answer

3. A pleasant climate
   B dangerous weapon
   C make a profet
   D sound the siren

4. A delishius meal
   B be effective
   C seem mysterious
   D negative attitude

5. A colorful bannar
   B chaos all around
   C gather together
   D filled with suspense

6. A various items
   B positive response
   C fabulous movie
   D nice and atractive

7. A empty gas tank
   B crowded hotel
   C a new display
   D valuable chrystal

8. A unlikely suspect
   B find a replacment
   C magazine renewal
   D strong reaction

9. A hungry moose
   B a school of goldfish
   C large cactus
   D injured the radias

10. A pleasent visit
    B funny comic strip
    C commit treason
    D bad habit

EXAMPLE

Ⓐ Ⓑ Ⓒ (D)

ANSWERS

1 Ⓐ Ⓑ Ⓒ Ⓓ

2 Ⓐ Ⓑ Ⓒ Ⓓ

3 Ⓐ Ⓑ Ⓒ Ⓓ

4 Ⓐ Ⓑ Ⓒ Ⓓ

5 Ⓐ Ⓑ Ⓒ Ⓓ

6 Ⓐ Ⓑ Ⓒ Ⓓ

7 Ⓐ Ⓑ Ⓒ Ⓓ

8 Ⓐ Ⓑ Ⓒ Ⓓ

9 Ⓐ Ⓑ Ⓒ Ⓓ

10 Ⓐ Ⓑ Ⓒ Ⓓ

Unit 5 Review *(continued)*
Practice Test: Part B

Are you <u>curias</u> and <u>clevor</u>? Do you have a <u>talint</u> for research? Then you might join the
     1   2   3

scientists who study the <u>enormos</u> number of <u>speces</u> of living things in the sea. These
                 4   5

scientists study even the <u>bakteria</u> and <u>fungie</u>. Study of the ocean is still <u>unpredictible</u>.
                6   7   8

Some research projects are <u>unsuccessful</u>, but there is little <u>disagreement</u> over the value
                 9   10

of ocean exploration.

The number of each set matches the number of an underlined word above. Mark the letter of the correctly spelled word.

1. **A** curiouse   **C** cureous
   B curiase   **D** curious

2. **A** clevir   **C** klever
   B clever   **D** clevver

3. **A** talant   **C** talont
   B tallent   **D** talent

4. **A** inormous   **C** enormous
   B enormouse   **D** enormus

5. **A** speceis   **C** speshies
   B species   **D** spicies

6. **A** bactera   **C** bacteria
   B bactiria   **D** backterra

7. **A** fungi   **C** funjie
   B funji   **D** fungy

8. **A** unpreditable   **C** unpridicible
   B unpredictable   **D** unpredicble

9. **A** unsucesfle   **C** unsuccessful
   B unsucessful   **D** unsuccesfal

10. **A** disagreement   **C** disagreemant
    B disagremant   **D** disagreemint

ANSWERS

1 (A) (B) (C) (D)
2 (A) (B) (C) (D)
3 (A) (B) (C) (D)
4 (A) (B) (C) (D)
5 (A) (B) (C) (D)
6 (A) (B) (C) (D)
7 (A) (B) (C) (D)
8 (A) (B) (C) (D)
9 (A) (B) (C) (D)
10 (A) (B) (C) (D)

Unit 5 Review *(continued)*
Activities

What's in a Word?

◆ *media*

Media looks like a singular word, but actually it is the plural form of the word *medium*. The word *medium* comes from Latin, and Latin nouns ending in *-um* have a plural ending in *-a*. Therefore, it is correct to say, "The *media* are critical of the mayor's new plan," not, "The *media* <u>is</u> critical of the mayor's new plan."

palace

The word *palace* dates from the time of Augustus Caesar, who built his home on one of the hills of Rome, Mons Palatinus. His imperial mansion was called a *palatium*.

sensitive

The word *sensitive* comes from *sensus*, a form of the Latin verb *sentire*, which means "to feel." A sensitive person can feel, react to, or appreciate something quickly and easily. Another word that comes from the same Latin root is *sensation*.

ROUND ROBIN

In a small group, write a round-robin story using the Unit Spelling Words. As the paper is passed around, each person adds a sentence to the story. The sentence should include one Spelling Word that hasn't been used in the story before. Keep passing the paper around until all the Spelling Words have been used.

Suspenseful Titles

Stories that are suspenseful often have titles that suggest a mystery or some danger. Work in a small group, and make up titles for suspenseful stories. Use some of the Spelling Words.

Select Some Words

Write five Spelling Words that you believe are difficult to spell. Challenge a classmate to spell the words. Then have the same classmate ask you to spell the words on his or her list of most difficult words.

YOUR OWN USAGE NOTES

With a partner, select four Spelling Words. Write usage notes—explanations or reminders for using words—for each of those words, with a reminder or an explanation of the correct current usage. (You may want to refer to a dictionary or another reference work.) Share your usage notes with the rest of the class.

◆ This indicates a Unit Spelling Word.

Unit 5 Review *(continued)*
Activities

Play charades

Work with a small group, and make a set of cards, each with a Spelling Word on it. Begin with the words on your lists and add other words. Put all the cards together, face down on a table. Take turns drawing a card from the pile, reading the word silently, and then acting it out. The others in the group try to guess the word.

STORY DICTATION

Make a list of five of your favorite words from this unit. Get together with a small group of classmates, and compare your list with their lists. Make one master list of all the words your group came up with. Then write a group story in which you try to use all the words on your master list. Share your group's story with the rest of the class.

Proofreading Partners

Do this activity with a partner. Each of you should make a list of five Spelling Words that give you trouble or that you consider challenging to spell correctly. Exchange lists. Write a paragraph on any topic you choose. Use your partner's five Spelling Words in your paragraph, but misspell them. Then exchange papers, and proofread and correct each other's paragraphs. Be sure each Spelling Word is spelled correctly.

What's in a Word?

suspense

Suspense is a word that can suggest doubt, worry, fear, or uncertainty. If you're "in suspense," you don't really know how something will turn out. Sometimes suspense is a pleasant state of mind, especially if you're watching or reading a mystery. Sometimes the feeling of being in suspense is not pleasant, especially if you're waiting for some news that might be bad.

◆ talent

The word *talent* originally meant a sum of money. It took on its present meaning because of the idea that someone who has a natural ability to do something is rich, as if he or she possessed a large sum of money.

unpredictable/dictionary

The word *unpredictable* and the word *dictionary* belong to the same word family. They share the word part *-dict-*, which comes from the Latin word *dicere*, meaning "to speak." Another word that belongs to the same word family is *contradict*.

◆ This indicates a Unit Spelling Word.

Lesson 30: Suffixes in Combination

Spelling Words

1. carefully
2. ownership
3. faithfully
4. peacefully
5. wonderfully
6. thoughtfully
7. relationship
8. respectively
9. naturally
10. nervously
11. gracefully
12. actively
13. joyfully
14. beautifully
15. successfully
16. accidentally

Each Spelling Word has two suffixes. Look at the words to see how the suffixes are spelled. Notice whether the spelling of the base word changes.

Sort the Spelling Words according to the suffixes. Use the headings in each list.

-fully
_____
_____
_____
_____
_____
_____
_____
_____

**-ively,
-ously, -ally**
_____
_____
_____
_____
_____
_____

**-ership,
-ionship**
_____
_____

Your Own Words

Find more words that have a combination of suffixes, and add them to the lists. In a video about dogs, you might hear words like *fearfully* and *joyously*. When might you use *incidentally* or *relatively*?

17. _____
18. _____
19. _____
20. _____

Sometimes spelling changes are made when suffixes are added to base words.

➤ **If a word ends with *y*, change the *y* to *i* before adding *-ly*.**

➤ **When a suffix that begins with a vowel is added to a base word that ends with *e*, the *e* is often dropped.**

Lesson 30: Suffixes in Combination *(continued)*

SPELLING CLUES: Suffixes Think about the rules for adding suffixes to words. Remember that some base words change their spelling when suffixes are added.

Check the two spellings in each pair. Write the correct spelling of each word.

1. relationship
   relateionship
2. joifully
   joyfully
3. ownership
   oanership

4. faithfully
   faithfuly
5. naturely
   naturally
6. activly
   actively

PROOFREADING 7–12. Proofread these sentences. Circle the misspelled word in each sentence. Then write the word correctly.

- If you are fearful and behave nerviously, a dog can sense it.
- To train a dog succesfuly, you may not be able to act naturally.
- See how bueatifully that dog obeys simple commands!
- He jumps so gracfully into the air to catch that stick.
- Then he carefuly places it at the trainer's feet.
- Dogs and people can get along wonderfly well, once a dog is trained.

FUN WITH WORDS Write a Spelling Word that fits the clue.

13. If you say "Oops!" you've probably done something this way.

14. If you settle an argument with a handshake, you have settled it in this way.

15. If you refer to two people in order, you refer to them this way.

16. To give the impression of speaking this way, an actor might touch his temple with his index finger and look serious.

1. _____
2. _____
3. _____
4. _____
5. _____
6. _____

7. _____
8. _____
9. _____
10. _____
11. _____
12. _____

13. _____
14. _____
15. _____
16. _____

Lesson 31: Prefix *in- (im-, il-, ir-)*

Spelling Words

1. *incomplete*
2. *informal*
3. *incorrect*
4. *independent*
5. *illegal*
6. *impolite*
7. *impossible*
8. *invisible*
9. *irregular*
10. *inexpensive*
11. *impure*
12. *inability*
13. *impatient*
14. *indigestion*
15. *indefinite*
16. *incredible*

Your Own Words

Look for other words with these prefixes to add to the lists. If you read a book about etiquette, you might read about *improper* and *inappropriate* behavior. When might you see *illogical* or *irrepressible?*

17. _____
18. _____
19. _____
20. _____

The prefix *in-* may be spelled *in-, im-, il-,* or *ir-*. This prefix gives each Spelling Word a negative meaning.

Sort the words in a way that will help you remember them. Two examples are given. Fill in the other two as you are sorting.

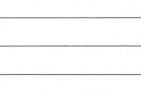

indirect

_____
_____
_____
_____
_____
_____
_____
_____
_____

impersonal

_____
_____
_____
_____
_____

_____   _____

The prefix *in- (im-, il-, ir-)* usually means "not." When this prefix is added to a word, the spelling of the base word does not change.

Lesson 31: Prefix *in-* *(im-, il-, ir-)* *(continued)*

SPELLING CLUES: Visual Clues When you're not sure how a word is spelled, try to remember how the word looks. Then write the word down. Does it look right?

Check the spelling of these words. Write the word if it looks correct. If the word does not look correct, write it correctly.

1. ilegal
2. imposible
3. inpatient

4. incorrect
5. independant
6. informal

1. _____
2. _____
3. _____
4. _____
5. _____
6. _____

PROOFREADING 7–12. Proofread this letter. Circle the misspelled words. Then write the words correctly.

Dear Trevor,
We've been here for two days now, and it is just increddible. I have found many fairly innexpencive gifts to take back home. My inabbility to speak the language makes it difficult to order food. I ordered something yesterday that gave me indigeston, but I'm fine now. I'm impatient with myself because I've made a few mistakes that caused me to appear impolit. My incompleat knowledge of the culture is my only excuse for this.

See you soon,
Jamie

7. _____
8. _____
9. _____
10. _____
11. _____
12. _____

WORKING WITH MEANING Write the Spelling Word with the opposite meaning of each definition.

13. free from germs or anything unhealthful
14. known for certain; plain and clear in meaning
15. able to be seen
16. always occurring at the same time

13. _____
14. _____
15. _____
16. _____

Lesson 32: Latin Roots *-scrib-/-script-*, *-spect-*

Spelling Words

1. inspect
2. suspect
3. scribe
4. script
5. descriptive
6. description
7. prescribed
8. inspector
9. spectacle
10. spectacular
11. scribbled
12. inscription
13. subscription
14. spectrum
15. spectators
16. transcripts

Your Own Words

Look for other words based on these Latin roots. You might see the words *manuscript* and *subscribe* in the front pages of a magazine. In writing about manners, you might use the word *respectful.*

17. _____
18. _____
19. _____
20. _____

Each Spelling Word has a Latin root. The root *-scrib-* or *-script-* comes from a Latin word meaning "to write." The root *-spect-* comes from a Latin word meaning "to look at."

Sort the words in a way that will help you remember them. An example word is given for each list.

-SCRIB- OR -SCRIPT- inscribe	-SPECT- respectable
_____	_____
_____	_____
_____	_____
_____	_____
_____	_____
_____	_____
_____	_____
_____	

When prefixes or suffixes are added to the Latin roots *-scrib-* or *-script-* and *-spect-*, the spelling of the root often remains the same.

Lesson 32: Latin Roots *-scrib-/-script-*, *-spect-*
(continued)

SPELLING CLUES: Comparing Spellings When you are unsure of how a word is spelled, write the word in each of the two or three ways you think it might be spelled. Then decide which spelling looks right to you.

Look at the three possible spellings for each word. Write the spelling that looks correct.

1. scribbled
   scribled
   skribbled

2. suspecked
   suspect
   suspekt

3. inspecter
   inspeckter
   inspector

4. subscribtion
   supscription
   subscription

5. transcripts
   transkripts
   transcribts

6. discription
   description
   describtion

PROOFREADING 7–12. Proofread the list of hints for travel. Circle the misspelled words. Then write each word correctly.

How to Get the Most out of Foreign Travel

- Read describtive articles about buildings and monuments.
- Read the description of the inskription on a historic landmark.
- Enjoy spectackular views of scenery.
- At sporting events, watch how spectadors behave.
- Take along the medicine the doctor preskribed.
- Carefully insspect any gifts before you buy them.

FUN WITH WORDS Write Spelling Words to match the descriptions.

13. If there were no typewriters and no computers, you might hire this person to write something for you.

14. An actor studies this to learn a role.

15. It's an event that's really something to see. You might describe it as an embarrassment, an extravaganza, or a contest.

16. This is what we call all the colors the eye can see.

1. _____
2. _____
3. _____
4. _____
5. _____
6. _____
7. _____
8. _____
9. _____
10. _____
11. _____
12. _____

13. _____
14. _____
15. _____
16. _____

Lesson 33: Latin Roots *-rupt-*, *-ject-*

Spelling Words

1. objected _____
2. projected _____
3. objections _____
4. projections _____
5. erupt _____
6. abrupt _____
7. bankrupt _____
8. inject _____
9. disrupting _____
10. disruption _____
11. eject _____
12. reject _____
13. rejected _____
14. rupture _____
15. corrupt _____
16. interrupt _____

Your Own Words

Look for words with these Latin roots to add to your lists. You might hear the words *project* and *object* in a science class. When might you use the word *eruption* in your writing?

17. _____
18. _____
19. _____
20. _____

Each Spelling Word has a Latin root. The root *-rupt-* comes from a Latin word meaning "to break." The root *-ject-* comes from a Latin word meaning "to throw."

Sort the words in a way that will help you remember them. Notice the spelling of each root as you are sorting.

-RUPT-

_____ _____
_____ _____
_____ _____
_____ _____

-JECT-

_____ _____
_____ _____
_____ _____
_____ _____

When prefixes or suffixes are added to the Latin roots *-rupt-* and *-ject-*, the spelling of the root often remains the same.

Lesson 33: Latin Roots *-rupt-*, *-ject-* *(continued)*

SPELLING CLUES: Roots When you need to spell a word with a Latin root, think about how the root is spelled. Then think about the sounds in the rest of the word before you try to spell the word.

Write the correctly spelled word in each pair.

1. disrupshin   disruption
2. ejekt   eject
3. erupt   eruped
4. objected   objeckted
5. projeckted   projected
6. rubture   rupture
7. objections   objecktions
8. bankrup   bankrupt

PROOFREADING 9–13. Proofread the paragraph. Circle the misspelled words and write each word correctly.

Life on the ship was becoming difficult for the young sailor. He knew better than to interupt when an officer gave an order. Still, he wished he could injeckt a few of his own ideas, but he was afraid someone would regect them. Also, he was afraid of disrubting the normal flow of events on board the ship. He objected to the abruptt manner of the captain and could hardly wait until the ship docked at a friendly port.

FUN WITH WORDS Write Spelling Words to replace 14–16.

1. _____
2. _____
3. _____
4. _____
5. _____
6. _____
7. _____
8. _____
9. _____
10. _____
11. _____
12. _____
13. _____
14. _____
15. _____
16. _____

How did this happen? My application was __14__ !

The old politicians are greedy and __15__ ! Vote them out!

The __16__ for the year are very good.

Unit 6 Review
Practice Test: Part A

Read the four possible spellings for each word. On the answer sheet, mark the letter of the correct spelling.

EXAMPLE:

A personul   C personal
B personil   D personel

1. A carfully   C carefuly
   B carefully   D carefuley

2. A activley   C activly
   B activeley   D actively

3. A ownurship   C ownership
   B ownershipe   D owner-ship

4. A illegal   C illegil
   B ilegal   D ilegel

5. A indefenite   C indefinite
   B indefanite   D indefenete

6. A independant   C indipendant
   B independent   D indipendent

7. A spectaculer   C spectacular
   B spectaculur   D spectecular

8. A subscripton   C sunscripion
   B subscription   D subscripshun

9. A projected   C projeckted
   B progected   D prajected

10. A corupt   C coroupt
    B corupe   D corrupt

EXAMPLE

(A) (B) (Ⓒ) (D)

ANSWERS

1 (A) (B) (C) (D)

2 (A) (B) (C) (D)

3 (A) (B) (C) (D)

4 (A) (B) (C) (D)

5 (A) (B) (C) (D)

6 (A) (B) (C) (D)

7 (A) (B) (C) (D)

8 (A) (B) (C) (D)

9 (A) (B) (C) (D)

10 (A) (B) (C) (D)

Unit 6 Review (continued)
Practice Test: Part B

Read each sentence. On the answer sheet, mark the letter
of the correctly spelled word.

EXAMPLE: The car _____.
A stopd   C stopped
B staped   D stopt

1. She read the _____.
   A scripte   C skript
   B script   D skrip

2. I'll _____ it.
   A inspect   C inspeckt
   B inspec   D inspet

3. Don't be _____.
   A impolyte   C inpolite
   B impulite   D impolite

4. The party is _____.
   A informel   C informal
   B imformal   D informle

5. Don't _____ it.
   A riject   C reject
   B regect   D rejeck

6. I _____ him.
   A suspeck   C subspect
   B suspect   D susspect

7. I danced _____.
   A joyfuly   C joyfaly
   B joyfally   D joyfully

8. Please don't _____ me.
   A interupt   C intarrupt
   B interup   D interrupt

9. The _____ is here.
   A skribe   C screib
   B scribe   D skreib

10. The oil is _____.
    A impur   C impure
    B impyur   D inpure

| EXAMPLE |
| A B (C) D |

| ANSWERS |
| 1 A B C D |
| 2 A B C D |
| 3 A B C D |
| 4 A B C D |
| 5 A B C D |
| 6 A B C D |
| 7 A B C D |
| 8 A B C D |
| 9 A B C D |
| 10 A B C D |

Unit 6 Review (continued)
Activities

What's in a Word?

bankrupt

The word *bankrupt* has a history that dates back to medieval times. At that time Italian moneylenders set up benches in the market area. They conducted their business from these benches. The Latin word for this type of bench is *banca*. If the moneylender's business failed, the bench had to be broken. The Latin expression for this process was *banca rupta*, which later became the English word *bankrupt*.

cordially

Cordially is an interesting word. It comes from the Latin root *cor*, which means "heart." When you thank someone who gave a party, you might mention his or her cordiality, which suggests that the hospitality came from the heart, or was heartfelt.

◆ incredible

The word *incredible* comes from the Latin word *credere*, which means "to believe." If something is incredible, it is not credible, or unbelievable. If an underdog team beats a championship team, sportscasters might call it "an incredible victory" because it comes as such a surprise.

The same Latin root is used in the word *credible*, which means "believable." When an underdog team beats a championship team, a credible explanation might be that the other team made a lot of mistakes.

◆ This indicates a Unit Spelling Word.

CHALLENGE YOURSELF

Choose five Spelling Words that you find difficult. When you have chosen your five words, write a sentence using each of them. Leave a blank where the Spelling Word belongs. Then, without looking at the Spelling Words, fill in the blanks, trying to spell the words correctly. When you are finished, check your spelling.

Pick a Card, Any Card

Work with a small group, and write each of the Spelling Words on a separate index card. Then place the cards face down on a table, mix them up, and take turns picking one. The person who picks the card says the word, spells it, and then uses it in a sentence.

Camping Partners

Do this activity with a partner. Each of you should write a paragraph about some kind of camping adventure. Use five Spelling Words in your paragraph, but don't write down the Spelling Words. Instead, leave blanks where the Spelling Words should go. Exchange papers, and fill in the five Spelling Words that are missing from your partner's paragraph. Then exchange papers again, and check each other's spelling.

Team Charades

Do this activity with at least three people on each team. Divide the Spelling Words so that each team has half of them. Each team writes on a slip of paper a clue—a familiar phrase, a book title, a movie title, a common saying—for each of their words. Then all slips are given to the other team. One at a time, each team member draws a slip, takes one minute to plan, and then acts out the clue for his or her team. When the word is guessed and then spelled correctly, it's the other team's turn. Play continues until all clues have been acted out and guessed.

NAME _____ CLASS _____ DATE _____

Unit 6 Review *(continued)*
Activities

Proofreading Partners

Do this activity with a partner. Each of you should make a list of five Spelling Words that give you trouble or that you need to think about before you spell them correctly. Exchange lists. Each partner should write a paragraph in which the other person's five words are misspelled. Then exchange papers, and proofread and correct each other's paragraphs. Be sure each Spelling Word is spelled correctly.

YOUR WORD HISTORIES

Have you kept up your collection of etymologies? Give it a twist by creating a section of Latin roots and Greek roots found in the Spelling Words and in other words you notice in your reading. Add these to your dictionary as well. Keep separate pages for words from Latin and from Greek.

A Final Scramble

Choose three Spelling Words and scramble the letters in each. Challenge a partner to unscramble the letters and spell each word correctly.

What's in a Word?

◆ *inexpensive* and *cheap*

The words *inexpensive* and *cheap* are close in meaning but are not quite the same. Both words mean that an object has a low price. *Inexpensive* suggests that the object has good value for its price: It is an *inexpensive* watch, but it keeps very good time. *Cheap* suggests that the object is not of the best quality: It was a *cheap* watch, and it stopped running shortly after I got it.

peace

The base word in *peacefully* is *peace*. Have you ever heard of the *Pax Romana*? This was a period in the history of the Roman Empire when there were no wars. *Pax* is the Latin word for *peace*. In French the word for *peace* is *paix,* and in Spanish it is *paz*. The South American country of Bolivia even has a city named La Paz.

◆ This indicates a Unit Spelling Word.

Unit 6 | Review | Lesson 34   79

Spelling Dictionary

This is the entry word. It's the word you look up.

These marks indicate the primary and secondary accents.

Look here to find out how to pronounce the entry word.

Here you'll find other forms of the entry word, such as the plural.

This abbreviation tells what part of speech the entry word is.*

This is a sample sentence using the entry word.

These are two definitions of the entry word.

This is the number of the lesson where you'll find the entry word.

Synonyms of the word are listed right after *syn*.

Use this key to help you figure out the sounds of the letters.

met·a·mor·pho·sis [met·ə·môr´fə·sis] *n.,* **metamorphoses 1.** In lower animals, a series of complete changes in body form that take place from birth to the adult stage. **2.** A complete or very obvious change: **We watched the** *metamorphosis* **of the tadpole into a frog.** *syns.* change, transformation [4]

Pronunciation Key

a	add, map	m	move, seem	u	up, done	
ā	ace, rate	n	nice, tin	û(r)	burn, term	
â(r)	care, air	ng	ring, song	yōō	fuse, few	
ä	palm, father	o	odd, hot	v	vain, eve	
b	bat, rub	ō	open, so	w	win, away	
ch	check, catch	ô	order, jaw	y	yet, yearn	
d	dog, rod	oi	oil, boy	z	zest, muse	
e	end, pet	ou	pout, now	zh	vision, pleasure	
ē	equal, tree	ŏŏ	took, full	ə	the schwa, an	
f	fit, half	ōō	pool, food		unstressed vowel	
g	go, log	p	pit, stop		representing the	
h	hope, hate	r	run, poor		sound spelled	
i	it, give	s	see, pass		a in **a**bout	
ī	ice, write	sh	sure, rush		e in list**e**n	
j	joy, ledge	t	talk, sit		i in penc**i**l	
k	cool, take	th	thin, both		o in mel**o**n	
l	look, rule	th	this, bathe		u in circ**u**s	

***Key to Abbreviations:** *n.* noun; *v.* verb; *adj.* adjective; *adv.* adverb; *prep.* preposition; *pron.* pronoun; *interj.* interjection; *conj.* conjunction; *syn.* synonym

Spelling Table

The sound	in	is spelled as—	The sound	in	is spelled as—
a	**a**dd	**ca**t, l**augh**, pl**ai**d	ō	**o**pen	**oh**, **o**ver, g**o**, **oa**k, gr**ow**, t**oe**, th**ough**, s**ou**l, s**ew**
ā	**a**ge	g**a**me, r**ai**n, d**ay**, g**augue**	ô	d**o**g	f**or**, m**ore**, r**oar**, b**a**ll, w**a**lk, d**aw**n, f**au**lt, br**oa**d, **ough**t
ä	p**a**lm	**ah**, f**a**ther, d**ar**k, h**ear**t			
â(r)	c**a**re	d**are**, f**air**, pr**ay**er, wh**ere**, b**ear**, th**eir**	oi	**oi**l	n**oi**se, t**oy**
b	**b**at	**b**ig, ca**b**in, ra**bb**it	o͝o	t**oo**k	f**oo**t, w**ou**ld, w**o**lf, p**u**ll
ch	**ch**eck	**ch**op, mar**ch**, ca**tch**, na**t**ure, men**t**ion	o͞o	p**oo**l	c**oo**l, l**o**se, s**ou**p, thr**ough**, r**u**de, d**ue**, fr**ui**t, dr**ew**, can**oe**
d	**d**og	**d**ig, ba**d**, la**dd**er, calle**d**			
e	**e**gg	**e**nd, m**e**t, r**ea**dy, **a**ny, s**ai**d, s**ay**s, fri**e**nd, b**u**ry, g**ue**ss	ou	**ou**t	**ou**nce, n**ow**, b**ough**
			p	**p**ut	**p**in, ca**p**, ha**pp**y
ē	**e**qual	sh**e**, **ea**t, s**ee**, p**eo**ple, k**ey**, f**ie**ld, ma**ch**ine, rec**ei**ve, p**ia**no, cit**y**	r	**r**un	**r**ed, ca**r**, hu**rr**y, **wr**ist, **rh**yme
f	**f**it	**f**ive, o**ff**er, cou**gh**, hal**f**, **ph**oto	s	**s**ee	**s**it, **sc**ene, lo**ss**, li**s**ten, **c**ity, p**s**ychology
g	**g**o	**g**ate, bi**gg**er, va**gue**, **gh**ost	sh	ru**sh**	**sh**oe, **s**ure, o**c**ean, spe**ci**al, ma**ch**ine, mi**ss**ion, lo**ti**on, pen**si**on, con**sci**ence
h	**h**ot	**h**ope, **wh**o			
i	**i**t	**i**nch, h**i**t, pr**e**tty, **e**mploy, b**ee**n, b**u**sy, g**ui**tar, dam**a**ge, w**o**men, m**y**th, h**e**re, d**ea**r	t	**t**op	**t**an, kep**t**, be**tt**er, walk**ed**, caugh**t**
			th	**th**in	**th**ink, clo**th**
ī	**i**ce	**i**tem, f**i**ne, p**ie**, h**igh**, b**uy**, tr**y**, d**ye**, **eye**, h**eigh**t, **i**sland, **ai**sle	t̶h̶	**th**is	**th**ese, clo**th**ing
			u	**u**p	c**u**t, b**u**tter, s**o**me, fl**oo**d, d**oe**s, y**ou**ng
j	**j**oy	**j**ump, **g**em, ma**g**ic, ca**ge**, e**dge**, sol**d**ier, gra**d**uate, exa**gg**erate	û(r)	b**ur**n	t**ur**n, b**ir**d, w**or**k, **ear**ly, j**our**ney, h**er**d
			v	**v**ery	**v**ote, o**v**er, o**f**
k	**k**eep	**k**ing, **c**at, lo**ck**, **ch**orus, a**cc**ount	w	**w**in	**w**ait, po**w**er
			y	**y**et	**y**ear, on**i**on
l	**l**ook	**l**et, ba**ll**	y͞o͞o	**u**se	**c**ue, f**ew**, **you**th, v**iew**, b**eau**tiful
m	**m**ove	**m**ake, ha**mm**er, ca**l**m, cli**mb**, conde**mn**			
n	**n**ice	**n**ew, ca**n**, fu**nn**y, **kn**ow, **gn**ome, **pn**eumonia	z	**z**oo	**z**ebra, la**z**y, bu**zz**, wa**s**, **sc**issors
			zh	vi**si**on	plea**s**ure, gara**g**e, televi**s**ion
ng	ri**ng**	thi**ng**, to**ngue**	ə		**a**bout, list**e**n, penc**i**l, mel**o**n, circ**u**s
o	**o**dd	p**o**t, h**o**nor			

A

a·bil·i·ty [ə·bil´ə·tē] *n.* the power or skill to do something: **An infant does not have the** *ability* **to talk.** [19]

a·brupt [ə·brupt´] *adj.* sudden and unexpected: **The bus came to an** *abrupt* **stop.** [33]

ab·sence [ab´səns] *n.* the fact of being not present: **The** *absence* **of the star player from the game was felt by the whole team.** [18]

ab·sent [ab´sənt] *adj.* not present: **Three students were** *absent* **from class.** [22]

ac·cept [ak·sept´] *v.* to take something that is offered or given: **Larry will** *accept* **the award next Monday.** [10]

ac·ci·dent [ak´sə·dənt] *n.* something bad or unlucky that happens unexpectedly: **Knocking the vase off the table was an** *accident.* [20]

ac·ci·den·tal·ly [ak´sə·den´təl·lē] *adv.* happening by accident: **The book was** *accidentally* **left out in the rain.** [30]

ac·com·pa·ny [ə·kum´pə·nē] *v.* to go with: **Heavy winds will** *accompany* **the rain.** [20]

ac·count [ə·kount´] *n.* a statement or record of how something happened: **She keeps an** *account* **of all her activities in her diary.** [3]

ac·cu·rate [ak´yər·it] *adj.* without errors or mistakes: **The police needed an** *accurate* **description of the suspect.** *syn.* correct [20]

ac·cuse [ə·kyōōz´] *v.* to say that someone has done something wrong or has committed a crime: **The police** *accuse* **the man of robbing the store.** [20]

ac·cus·tomed [ə·kus´təmd] *adj.* familiar or experienced with; used to: **She is not** *accustomed* **to speaking in public and gets nervous when she has to do it.** [20]

a·chieve [ə·chēv´] *v.* to do or carry out: **He will** *achieve* **his goals if he works hard.** [7]

ac·tive·ly [ak´tiv·lē] *adv.* in action; working: **My grandfather is** *actively* **involved with running the family business.** [30]

ac·tiv·i·ty [ak·tiv´ə·tē] *n., activities* 1. something that is done or to be done: **The children participate in many after-school** *activities.* 2. the state of being active; action; movement: **Their house was always full of** *activity.* [12, 19]

a·dapt [ə·dapt´] *v.* to change in order to fit into a new situation: **I hope the plants will** *adapt* **to their new environment.** [10]

ad·mire [ad·mīr´] *v.* to think highly of: **Many people** *admire* **the late Mother Teresa for her life of service to others.** *syn.* respect [14]

ad·mit [ad·mit´] *v., admitted* to say against one's will that something is true: **I don't like the way she shows off, but I** *admit* **she's a good player. Casey** *admitted* **that he broke the dish.** [1, 16]

a·dopt [ə·dopt´] *v.* to take another's child into one's family and raise as one's own: **Mrs. Allen wanted to** *adopt* **her grandchild after the baby's mother died.** [10]

ad·vance [ad·vans´] *v.* to move forward: **In football, a team must** *advance* **the ball ten yards to get a first down.** [1]

af·fair [ə·fâr´] *n.* an action or occasion: **Jake wore a tuxedo to the formal** *affair.* [20]

af·fect [ə·fekt´] *v.* to make a difference in: **I hope that this misunderstanding won't** *affect* **our friendship.** [10]

af·fec·tion [ə·fek´shən] *n.* a feeling of liking or friendship: **On Valentine's Day, flowers, cupids, and hearts are often symbols of** *affection.* [20]

a·gent [ā´jənt] *n.* a person who does business for others: **A real estate** *agent* **helps people to buy or sell their homes.** [15]

al·lied [ə·līd´ or al´īd] *adj.* joined or connected in some way: **Great Britain and the United States were** *allied* **against Germany in World War II.** [12]

al·low·ance [ə·lou´əns] *n.* a sum of money set aside for a certain purpose: **I was given a weekly** *allowance* **if I completed all my chores.** [18]

al·though [ôl·thō´] *conj.* in spite of: **We were able to complete the game** *although* **it rained right up to the last minute.** [6]

am·bu·lance [am´byə·ləns] *n.* a specially equipped vehicle that carries the sick or wounded: **Cars must pull over to the curb to make way for an** *ambulance.* [18]

A·mer·i·can [ə·mer´ə·kən] *adj.* **1.** having to do with the United States: **The** *American* **flag is a symbol of patriotism. 2.** having to do with North or South America: **There are two** *American* **continents, North America and South America.** [13]

a·mong [ə·mung´] *prep.* in the middle of: **She found herself** *among* **a crowd of people.** [6]

a·mount [ə·mount´] *n.* a number or quantity: **I have managed to save a small** *amount* **of money.** [3]

an·gel [ān´jəl] *n.* **1.** in some religions, a heavenly being or spirit: **The painting showed an** *angel* **watching over the child. 2.** a person who is thought of as being very good: **Joe behaves like a little** *angel* **when his mother is around.** [10]

an·gle [āng´gəl] *n.* the area formed by two straight lines or flat surfaces that join at a given point: **There are ninety degrees in a right** *angle.* [10]

an·swer [an´sər] *v.* to speak or write in reply: **Susan** *answered* **every question on the quiz.** [16]

a·part [ə·pärt´] *adv.* away from each other in space or time: **Timmy had to stay** *apart* **from the other children until he could behave.** *syn.* separate [4]

ap·par·ent [ə·pâr´ənt] *adj.* plain to see: **There was no** *apparent* **reason for his behavior.** *syn.* obvious [20]

ap·pear·ance [ə·pir´əns] *n.* the way a person or thing looks: **Grandma was surprised by Megan's grown-up** *appearance.* [18]

ap·plause [ə·plôz´] *n.* approval or enjoyment shown by the clapping of hands: **The audi-ence burst into** *applause* **at the end of the performance.** [20]

ap·ply [ə·plī´] *v.,* **applies** to put on: **The clown carefully** *applies* **the face paint.** [12]

ap·point [ə·point´] *v.* to name a person to a job or position: **The principal** *appointed* **three teachers to a special committee.** [20]

ap·pre·ci·ate [ə·prē´shē·āt´] *v.* to realize the worth or value of something: **I'd like you to know how much we** *appreciate* **all the help that you've given us.** [20]

ap·proach [ə·prōch´] *v.* to come nearer to: **The lawyers** *approach* **the bench so that the judge can speak to them privately.** [20]

a·pron [ā´prən] *n.* a piece of material tied loosely around the body to protect clothing: **The chef took off his** *apron* **when he left the kitchen.** [15]

ar·gu·ment [är´gyə·mənt] *n.* a disagreement or quarrel; dispute: **They became angry during their discussion about politics, and the discussion turned into an** *argument.* [19]

as·sem·bly [ə·sem´blē] *n.* the gathering together of a group of people: **There was an** *assembly* **the first week of school to inform the students about the new safety rules.** [20]

as·sign [ə·sīn´] *v.* to give out work: **The teacher said that he would** *assign* **only ten prob-lems for our math homework.** [20]

as·sis·tance [ə·sis´təns] *n.* the act of helping: **The truck driver stopped to give** *assistance* **to the stranded motorist.** *syn.* aid [20]

Pronunciation Key

a	add	ō	open	th	thin
ā	ace	ô	off	th	this
â(r)	care	oi	oil	zh	vision
ä	palm	ŏŏ	took		
e	end	ōō	pool	ə	a in about
ē	equal	ou	out		e in listen
i	it	u	up		i in pencil
ī	ice	û(r)	burn		o in melon
o	odd	yōō	use		u in circus

as·sis·tant [ə·sis´tənt] *n.* any person who gives help or support: **Since the store manager is not here today, her** *assistant* **is in charge.** *syn.* helper [22]

as·so·ci·a·tion [ə·sō´s(h)ē·ā´shən] *n.* an organization of people who work together for a common purpose: **Ms. Bryant belongs to a professional** *association* **related to her job.** [20]

as·sur·ance [ə·shŏŏr´əns] *n.* a statement made to inspire confidence: **The salesclerk gave us his** *assurance* **that the stain remover would take out the spot.** [18]

at·trac·tive [ə·trak´tiv] *adj.* having the power to attract someone or something; pleasing to look at or think about: **The salesclerk made me an** *attractive* **offer on the car.** [27]

au·di·ence [ô´dē·əns] *n.* a group of people who watch a certain event: **The** *audience* **stood to applaud the violinist's performance.** [18]

au·thor·i·ty [ə·thôr´ə·tē] *n.* the power or right to act, command, or make decisions: **Only Congress, not the President of the United States, has the** *authority* **to declare war on another country.** [19]

B

bac·te·ria [bak·tir´ē·ə] *n., pl.; n., s.* **bac·te·ri·um** single-celled organisms that can be seen only under a microscope: **Some kinds of** *bacteria* **cause diseases, but other kinds are helpful.** [26]

bait [bāt] *n.* something used to attract fish or other animals so they can be caught: **I like to go fishing with Dad, but he always has to put the** *bait* **on my hook.** [2]

bank·rupt [bangk´rupt] *adj.* unable to pay one's bills: **During a recession, many companies may become** *bankrupt* **and go out of business.** [33]

ban·ner [ban´ər] *n.* cloth with letters or pictures that represent something: **The drum major marched at the head of the band, waving the school** *banner.* [25]

bare·foot [bâr´fŏŏt´] *adv.* without shoes: **I love to walk** *barefoot* **along the beach.** [8]

ba·sis [bā´sis] *n.* an important idea that supports or proves something: **What is the** *basis* **of your claim that students who watch a lot of television get poor grades?** [15]

beat [bēt] *v.,* **beaten** to defeat: **The pennant winner was** *beaten* **by the last-place team.** [13]

beau·ti·ful·ly [byŏŏ´tə·fəl·lē] *adv.* in a pleasing way: **That musician plays the violin** *beautifully.* [30]

bed·time [bed´tīm´] *n.* a time to go to bed: **My little brother always finds something he needs to do just before** *bedtime.* [8]

be·lief [bə·lēf´] *n.* an idea held in the mind and thought to be true: **There's a popular** *belief* **that a person can catch a cold from getting chilled.** [7]

bis·cuit [bis´kit] *n.* a small baked roll made from flour and baking powder, baking soda, or yeast: **A breakfast of a** *biscuit* **and eggs is popular in some parts of the country.** [6]

bod·y·guard [bod´ē·gärd] *n.* someone whose job is to protect another person: **When the Prince of Wales travels to another country, he is protected by a** *bodyguard.* [8]

boul·der [bōl´dər] *n.* a large, rounded rock that rests above or partly above the ground: **A** *boulder* **is usually shaped and weathered by natural forces.** [6]

boy·friend [boi´frend´] *n.* a favorite male companion: **Gina went to a movie with her new** *boyfriend.* [7]

brag [brag] *v.,* **bragged** to boast about oneself: **Ken** *bragged* **about what a great catch he made at last week's game.** [16]

breathe [br<u>ea</u>th] *v.* to take air into the lungs and let it out: **You should** *breathe* **deeply when you exercise.** [2]

bride [brīd] *n.* a woman who is about to be married or is just married: **The** *bride* **wore a white satin dress with a long train.** [2]

build·ing [bil´ding] *n.* a structure with walls and a roof: **I wonder what use the city is going to make of the old library** *building*. [6]

burnt [bûrnt] *adj.* scorched or changed by fire or heat: **Our toaster doesn't work right, so we had** *burnt* **toast for breakfast.**—*v.* an alternative past tense and past participle of burn: **Gary** *burnt* **his finger when he touched the hot stove.** [4]

bus·y [biz´ē] *adj.* engaged in some activity or operation: **Janie's line was** *busy,* **and I had to call back.** [6]

C

cac·tus [kak´təs] *n., pl.* **cac·ti** [kak´tī] a plant with a thick green trunk and spines or bristles instead of leaves: **The** *cactus* **can store water in its trunk.** [26]

care·ful·ly [kâr´fəl·lē] *adv.* paying close attention; using care: **He drove** *carefully* **on the slick, ice-covered roads.** [30]

cen·tu·ry [sen´chə·rē] *n.,* **centuries** any period of 100 years: **There have been many scientific discoveries during the past two** *centuries.* [12]

cham·pi·on·ship [cham´pē·ən·ship´] *n.* the position of winning; being a champion: **Joe Louis held the heavyweight boxing** *championship* **of the world longer than any other person.** [19]

cha·os [kā´os] *n.* great confusion and disorder: **There was complete** *chaos* **when the storm knocked out the electricity all over the city.** [25]

chee·tah [chē´tə] *n.* a wild cat with spots like a leopard: **The** *cheetah* **can run faster than any other animal.** [15]

cit·y [sit´ē] *n.,* **cities** a large area in which many people live and work: **Paris is one of the most beautiful** *cities* **in the world.** [12]

clev·er [klev´ər] *adj.* showing skill or quick thinking: **That was** *clever* **of Alice to fasten her skirt with a paper clip until she could find a pin.** [25]

cli·mate [klī´mit] *n.* the usual weather that a place or region has: **Southern California has a sunny and mild** *climate.* [24]

col·o·ny [kol´ə·nē] *n.,* **colonies** a group of people who live in a land that is ruled by another country: **In 1776, the American** *colonies* **rebelled against English rule.** [12]

com·ic [kom´ik] *adj.* funny or amusing: **Charlie Chaplin often played a character who was both** *comic* **and sad.** [24]

com·mand [kə·mand´] *v.* to direct the course or actions of: **George Washington** *commanded* **the American army in the Revolutionary War.** [21]

com·man·der [kə·man´dər] *n.* a leader; a person in command: **The President of the United States is the** *Commander* **in Chief of the country's armed forces.** [21]

com·mence [kə·məns´] *v.* to go into action: **The work will** *commence* **as soon as the contract is signed.** *syns.* begin, start [21]

Pronunciation Key

a	add	ō	open	th	thin
ā	ace	ô	off	<u>th</u>	this
â(r)	care	oi	oil	zh	vision
ä	palm	o͝o	took		
e	end	o͞o	pool	ə	a in about
ē	equal	ou	out		e in listen
i	it	u	up		i in pencil
ī	ice	û(r)	burn		o in melon
o	odd	yo͞o	use		u in circus

com·ment [kom´ent] *n.* an idea expressed in speech or writing: **The senator made a *comment* about the situation in the Middle East.** [1]

com·mer·cial [kə·mûr´shəl] *n.* an advertisement on television or radio: **Professional football games on TV often have at least one *commercial* for cars or trucks.** [21]

com·mit [kə·mit´] *v.*, **committed** to pledge; to make known one's view: **Maria said she would *commit* to selling the goods at the bake sale. Bob *committed* all his spare time to the fund drive.** [16, 21]

com·mit·tee [kə·mit´ē] *n.* a group of people who work together for a common purpose: **Diane worked with the *committee* to plan a holiday party.** [21]

com·mon·ly [kom´ən·lē] *adv.* happening or appearing often; not rare or unusual: **Wolves were once *commonly* found in many parts of the world, but they now live in only a few places.** *syns.* ordinarily, usually [21]

com·mo·tion [kə·mō´shən] *n.* a noisy and loud disturbance: **The two dogs began chasing each other around the house and created quite a *commotion*.** [21]

com·mu·ni·cate [kə·myoo´nə·kāt´] *v.* to share information, feelings, or thoughts: **The head football coach used a phone so that he could *communicate* directly with his assistant coach in the press box.** [21]

com·mu·ni·ca·tion [kə·myoo´nə·kā´shən] *n.* the act of communicating or what is communicated: **Mom gave me postcards so she would get some *communication* from me while I was away at camp.** [21]

com·mu·ni·ty [kə·myoo´nə·tē] *n.*, **communities** a group of people who live in the same area, such as a neighborhood or town, or the area itself: **Most of the people in that *community* live in one-family homes. We are joining with the neighboring *communities* to oppose the installation of new, brighter streetlights.** [19, 21]

con·fer·ence [kon´fər·əns] *n.* a meeting to discuss something: **Mom had a *conference* with my teacher to discuss my progress in school.** [18]

con·fi·dent [kon´fə·dənt] *adj.* believing strongly: **Hal knew the answers to all the questions, so he's *confident* he'll get an A on the test.** *syns.* sure, certain [22]

con·fus·ing [kən·fyooz´ing] *adj.* disordered or mixed up: **The directions for assembling this dollhouse are very *confusing*.** [21]

con·sid·er [kən·sid´ər] *v.* to think about carefully: **I can't give you an answer until I've *considered* all the information.** [21]

con·sti·tu·tion [kon´stə·t(y)oo´shən] *n.* the basic principles and laws on which the government of a state or nation is based: **In some states students in the ninth grade study their state *constitution*.** [21]

con·tact [kon´takt] *n.* the act of coming together or touching: **The plane's landing was very smooth, and we barely felt the wheels come into *contact* with the ground.**—*v.* to get in touch with; communicate with: **Mom will *contact* all the players on my team by phone to tell them the time of the game.** [1]

con·tin·ue [kən·tin´yoo] *v.* to keep on with some activity or process: **The news story began on page one of the paper and *continued* on page twelve.** [21]

con·tract [kon´trakt] *n.* an agreement, usually written, that has the force of law: **The baseball player signed a five-year *contract* with the Yankees.** [1]

con·vic·tion [kən·vik´shən] *n.* a strong belief about something: **The experiment failed, but the scientist had the absolute *conviction* that his theory was right.** [21]

con·vince [kən·vins´] *v.* to make a person believe or do something: **I am sure you can *convince* Charlie that going to college is a good idea.** [14]

cool [kool] *v.* to make something less warm: **The pie is *cooling* on the kitchen table.** [16]

cor·rupt [kə·rupt´] *adj.* having poor morals; not honest: **The *corrupt* politician was voted out of office because of his dishonesty.** *syn.* dishonest [33]

cos·tume [kos´t(y)o͞om] *n.* clothes worn to dress up like someone or something else: **Annie wore a pirate *costume* for the party.** [10]

count [kount] *v.* to name or write numbers in order: **Can you *count* backward from one hundred?** [3]

coun·ty [koun´tē] *n.* one of the sections into which a state or country is divided: **A *county* has its own local government.** [3]

cour·age [kûr´ij] *n.* the quality of being able to face danger or pain without giving in to fear: **Soldiers in battle often display great *courage*.** *syn.* bravery [6]

crawl [krôl] *v.* to move slowly on the hands and knees: **The baby rocked back and forth on her hands and knees for a long time before she actually *crawled*.** [3]

creak [krēk] *v.* to make a sharp, squeaking sound: **The steps *creak* as he climbs them.** [9]

cre·a·tive [krē·ā´tiv] *adj.* good at making new things or having new ideas: **Will is fun to work with because he has such a *creative* mind.** [27]

creek [krēk] *n.* a stream smaller than a river and larger than a brook: **The boys went down to the *creek* to go fishing.** [9]

crim·i·nal [krim´ə·nəl] *n.* a person who is guilty of breaking the law: **The judge sentenced the *criminal* to two years in prison.** [13]

crit·i·cal [krit´i·kəl] *adj.* **1.** looking for faults: **He is very *critical* and seldom says a good thing about anyone. 2.** related to a crisis; crucial: **High school juniors and seniors must make *critical* decisions about their futures.** [13]

cross [krôs] *v.* to go from one side of something to another: **Don't *cross* the street in the middle of the block.** [3]

crys·tal [kris´təl] *n.* vases, plates, and other things made from a fine, clear glass: **Mom won't let us dry her good *crystal* because she's afraid we'll break it.** [25]

cup·board [kub´ərd] *n.* a cabinet with shelves used to store food, dishes, and other items: **The jam is on the second shelf of the *cupboard* next to the stove.** [8]

curb [kûrb] *n.* the raised concrete edge of a street: **The *curb* is painted yellow, which means we can't park there.** [4]

cu·ri·os·i·ty [kyo͝or´ē·os´ə·tē] *n.* a feeling of wanting to know more about something: **Two-year-old children have great *curiosity* and are always touching and tasting things.** [19]

cu·ri·ous [kyo͝or´ē·əs] *adj.* **1.** very interested in finding out about things and people: **A good scientist must have a *curious* mind. 2.** strange and unusual: **That was a *curious* thing to say.** [27]

cur·rent [kûr´ənt] *adj.* belonging to the present time: **She moved out of town last year, and I don't know her *current* address.** [22]

cus·tom [kus´təm] *n.* the way things are usually done by people in general: **In some countries, it is the *custom* to take a nap during the hottest time of the day.** [10]

Pronunciation Key

a	add	ō	open	th	thin
ā	ace	ô	off	th	this
â(r)	care	oi	oil	zh	vision
ä	palm	o͝o	took		
e	end	o͞o	pool	ə	a in about
ē	equal	ou	out		e in listen
i	it	u	up		i in pencil
ī	ice	û(r)	burn		o in melon
o	odd	yo͞o	use		u in circus

de·cent [dē´sənt] *adj.* accepted by people as proper and respectable: **Our new neighbor, Jenny, seems like a kind and *decent* person.** [10]

de·clare [di·klâr´] *v.* to announce in a formal way: **We are going to *declare* Joan the winner.** [4]

de·li·cious [di·lish´əs] *adj.* tasting very good: **The fresh fruit tasted *delicious*.** [27]

de·ny [di·nī´] *v.*, **denied** to say something is not true: **The accused man *denied* that he had been in the store at the time of the robbery.** [12]

depth [depth] *n.* how deep something is: **The divers went down into the water to a *depth* of fifty feet.** [1]

de·scent [di·sent´] *n.* the act of moving from a higher to a lower place: **We had to fasten our seat belts when the plane began its *descent* to the airport.** [10]

de·scrip·tion [di·skrip´shən] *n.* an account of how something or someone looked, felt, or acted, or how an event took place: **The witness was able to give the police an accurate *description* of the robber.** [32]

de·scrip·tive [di·skrip´tiv] *adj.* serving to describe: **We have to write a *descriptive* paragraph for English class.** [32]

de·vice [di·vīs´] *n.* a small tool or machine: **A blender is a *device* that cuts and mixes foods.** [10]

de·vise [di·vīz´] *v.* to think up: **The spies *devise* a plan to smuggle a secret message out of the country.** [10]

dif·fer·ence [dif´(ə·)rəns] *n.* the fact of being unlike someone or something else: **There's a *difference* between the way that actor looks in the movies and the way he looks in real life.** [18]

dis·a·gree·a·ble [dis´ə·grē´ə·bəl] *adj.* hard to get along with; bad or unpleasant: **Joey feels *disagreeable* this morning because he didn't get enough sleep last night.** [28]

dis·a·gree·ment [dis´ə·grē´mənt] *n.* the act of disagreeing: **They had a bitter *disagreement* and no longer speak to each other.** [28]

dis·play [dis·plā´] *n.* the act of showing something: **His *display* of anger frightened me.** [25]

dis·rupt [dis·rupt´] *v.* to put out of order; break up: **As the teacher tried to explain the problem, one boy kept *disrupting* the lesson by talking and jumping out of his seat.** *syns.* upset; disturb [33]

dis·rup·tion [dis·rup´shən] *n.* the act of breaking up; interference: **The storm caused a *disruption* of electrical power.** [33]

dough [dō] *n.* a mixture of flour, liquid, and other ingredients used to make bread, cookies, and other foods: **When Dad makes bread, he puts the *dough* in a warm place to rise.** [6]

ea·ger [ē´gər] *adj.* wanting to do or have something very much: **They enjoyed their day at the beach and are *eager* to go back again soon.** [15]

ef·fect [i·fekt´] *n.* something that happens because of something else: **The ointment I put on my rash had an immediate *effect*, and the itching has stopped.** [10]

ef·fec·tive [i·fek´tiv] *adj.* having an effect; able to change or influence something: **Dr. Martin Luther King, Jr., was an *effective* speaker.** [27]

eighth [āth] *adj.* next after the seventh; 8th: **The Yankees will be playing the outfield in the *eighth* inning; they are infield now in the seventh inning.** [6]

e·ject [i·jekt´] *v.* to throw or push out: **The manager will *eject* from the theater anyone who keeps talking.** [33]

e·lec·tric·i·ty [i·lek´tris´ə·tē] *n.* a basic form of energy that comes from the way certain tiny particles move: *Electricity* **is used to provide power for lights, motors, and many other devices.** [19]

el·e·ment [el´ə·mənt] *n.* **1.** any one of the basic substances from which all other things are made: **Iron is a basic** *element* **in nature. 2.** one of the basic parts of something: **The** *element* **of suspense is necessary in a good mystery story.** [22]

el·e·phant [el´ə·fənt] *n.* a large mammal with a long trunk and floppy ears: **The** *elephant* **is the largest of all land animals.** [22]

emp·ty [emp´tē] *adj.* lacking what could or should be present; without the usual contents: **Can you find an** *empty* **box somewhere that I could use as a place to keep my baseball cards?** [25]

en·e·my [en´ə·mē] *n.,* **enemies** someone who fights or acts against another, especially in a war: **The United States and Germany were** *enemies* **in World War II.** [12]

en·gine [en´jin] *n.* a machine that uses energy to make something move: **The mechanic raised the hood to look at the car's** *engine.* [14]

e·nor·mous [i·nôr´məs] *adj.* extremely large; much bigger than usual: **Some kinds of dinosaurs were** *enormous* **animals.** *syn.* huge [27]

e·nough [i·nuf´] *adj.* just the right amount: **I hope we have** *enough* **food for everyone who comes to the party.** [6]

en·trance [en´trəns] *n.* **1.** a door or passage through which one enters a place: **The** *entrance* **to the park is on Pine Street. 2.** the act of entering: **The dancer slipped as she made her** *entrance.* [18]

e·rupt [i·rupt´] *v.* to burst violently: **When volcanoes** *erupt,* **hot rushing lava can bury cities.** [33]

es·cape [i·skāp´] *n.* the act or fact of breaking out or getting free: **The soldiers planned a daring** *escape* **from the prison camp.** [14]

eth·nic [eth´nik] *adj.* having to do with people who have the same background: **Irish Americans and Mexican Americans are among the** *ethnic* **groups living in the United States.** [1]

e·vil [ē´vəl] *adj.* very bad: **Some aspects of the crime scene were so** *evil,* **the details were not released to the public.** *syn.* wicked [15]

ex·cel·lent [ek´sə·lənt] *adj.* of very high quality; outstanding: **Nineteen correctly answered questions out of twenty is an** *excellent* **score on a test.** [22]

ex·cept [ik·sept´] *prep.* leaving out; other than: **None of the players in soccer are allowed to use their hands** *except* **the goalie.** [10]

ex·ec·u·tive [ig·zek´yə·tiv] *n.* a person who manages or helps manage a business or organization: **A vice president of a company is an** *executive.*—*adj.* having to do with an executive: **An** *executive* **decision was made to sell more company stock.** [27]

ex·plor·er [ik·splôr´ər] *n.* a person who goes to a new or unknown place to learn about it; a person who explores: **Francisco de Coronado was a Spanish** *explorer* **in North America.** [13]

Pronunciation Key

a	add	ō	open	th	thin
ā	ace	ô	off	th	this
â(r)	care	oi	oil	zh	vision
ä	palm	ŏŏ	took		
e	end	ōō	pool	ə	a in about
ē	equal	ou	out		e in listen
i	it	u	up		i in pencil
ī	ice	û(r)	burn		o in melon
o	odd	yōō	use		u in circus

F

fab·u·lous [fab´yə·ləs] *adj.* like a fable or story; very great or extreme; beyond belief: **They must have had to pay a *fabulous* amount of money to build such a beautiful house.** *syn.* amazing [27]

fair·y tale [fâr´ē·tāl´] *n.* a very old story involving imaginary beings such as fairies, magicians, and dragons: **"Sleeping Beauty" is one of several famous *fairy tales* about a girl who marries a handsome prince.** [8]

faith·ful·ly [fāth´fəl·ē] *adv.* in a faithful way; with devotion: **The little dog trotted *faithfully* at the side of its owner.** *syn.* loyally [30]

fam·i·ly [fam´ə·lē] *n.*, **families 1.** a unit of one or more parents and their children: **Most of the *families* in our neighborhood have more than one child. 2.** a group of persons forming a household: **My roommate and I don't have relatives living nearby so we consider each other *family*.** [12]

fa·mous [fā´məs] *adj.* well known to many people: **Some *famous* athletes appear at events to raise money for charity.** [15]

fa·tal [fāt´(ə)l] *adj.* causing death: **The newscaster reported a *fatal* fire located five blocks from where I live.** *syn.* deadly [25]

fi·ber [fī´bər] *n.* **1.** a threadlike piece of material: **Cotton is a type of *fiber* used in making clothing. 2.** a kind of food that is coarse in texture: **Doctors recommend that people eat a diet high in *fiber*.** [15]

fierce [firs] *adj.* likely to attack; dangerous: **A tiger is a *fierce* animal.** [7]

fif·teen [fif´tēn´] *n., adj.* the number that is one more than fourteen; 15: **My younger sister is turning *fifteen* today.** [14]

fire·works [fīr´wûrks´] *n.* firecrackers, rockets, and other explosives that make a lot of noise and fill the sky with colored lights: **I like to see the *fireworks* on the Fourth of July.** [8]

for·eign [fôr´in] *adj.* away from one's own country; relating to another country: **He is English but he can speak two *foreign* languages, French and German.** [7]

fran·tic [fran´tik] *adj.* very excited because of fear, worry, or anger: **They were *frantic* when they thought their little boy was lost.** [14]

freight [frāt] *n.* goods moved by plane, ship, truck, or train: **Dave's father drives a truck that carries *freight* from one coast to the other.** [7]

Fri·day [frī´dē] *n.* the sixth day of the week: **On *Friday*, we always have a spelling test.** [15]

friend·ship [frend´ship´] *n.* the feeling between friends: **Grandmother's *friendship* with Marilyn began when they were both children.** [19]

frig·id [frij´id] *adj.* extremely cold; freezing cold: **The area near the North Pole has *frigid* weather conditions.** [24]

fun·gus [fun´gəs] *n.*, **fungi** [fun´jī´] one of a large group of plants without flowers or leaves: **Mushrooms and mold are types of *fungi*.** [26]

fun-lov·ing [fun´luv·ing] *adj.* easygoing; liking to have a good time: **Dick is a *fun-loving* boy who never seems to take anything seriously.** [8]

fun·nel [fun´əl] *n.* a cone-shaped utensil used to pour liquid into a container with a small opening: **The farmer poured cider through a *funnel* into the bottle.** [25]

fur·ther [fûr´thər] *adv.* to a greater degree; more: **She doesn't think there is any reason to discuss the matter any *further*.** [14]

G

gath·er [gath´ər] *v.* to pick up or collect: **They will *gather* some wood from the forest for their fire.** [25]

Ger·man [jûr´mən] *adj.* having to do with Germany or the German language: *Nein* is the *German* word for "no." [13]

get [get] *v.,* **gotten** to obtain or acquire: **I have *gotten* a new pair of skates to replace my old ones.** [14]

girl·friend [gûrl´frend´] *n.* a favorite female companion: **Clark is growing a mustache to impress his new *girlfriend.*** [7]

glance [glans] *v.* to look at something quickly and briefly: **The man did *glance* back to be sure no one was following him.** [1]

globe [glōb] *n.* **1.** any object or shape that is round like a ball: **The electric lamp had the shape of a *globe.*** **2.** a round object, usually hollow, on which a map of the earth or sky is drawn: **Jay pointed to the United States on the *globe.*** [2]

gold·fish [gōld´fish´] *n., pl.* **goldfish** a small fish that usually has an orange-gold color: **People often keep *goldfish* in home aquariums.** [26]

go·pher [gō´fər] *n.* a small, furry animal that lives in tunnels it burrows in the ground: **The *gopher* is a North American animal.** [24]

grace·ful·ly [grās´fəl·lē] *adv.* showing or having grace; done in a smooth, easy, and beautiful way: **The ballet dancer moved *gracefully* across the stage.** [30]

green·house [grēn´hous´] *n.* a glass or plastic building with a controlled temperature, used for growing plants all year round: **Florists grow beautiful flowers in a *greenhouse.*** [8]

groan [grōn] *v.* to make a deep, sad sound when one is in pain, unhappy, or upset: **The students will *groan* when they hear there is a surprise quiz today.** *syn.* moan [9]

gross [grōs] *adj.* with nothing taken out; complete: **A person's *gross* pay is the amount he or she is paid before taxes and other fees are taken out.**—*n.* twelve dozen: **She counted exactly 144 pencils in the *gross.*** [2]

grove [grōv] *n.* a group of trees standing together: **While in Florida, we drove by a huge orange *grove.*** [2]

grow [grō] *v.,* **grown** to increase in size or age: **David has *grown* almost six inches in the past year.** [9]

guess [ges] *v.* to have an idea without being sure that it is right: **He didn't study at all for the test and just *guessed* at most of the answers.** [9]

guest [gest] *n.* a person who visits another person's home: **Mom said I should serve my *guest* before taking any food myself.** [9]

H

hab·it [hab´it] *n.* something that is done so often or so long that one does it without thinking: **Chad has a bad *habit* of biting his nails.** [25]

heal [hēl] *v.* to make well or become well: **Over time, the cut on his arm *healed.*** [16]

heights [hīts] *n.* a high place: **She wouldn't look over the edge of the cliff because she is afraid of *heights.*** [7]

hip·po·pot·a·mus [hip´ə·pot´ə·məs] *n., pl.* **hip·po·pot·a·mus·es** [hip´ə·pot´ə·məs·əs] or **hip·po·pot·a·mi** [hip´ə·pot´əmī] a big, heavy animal with short legs, a large head, and thick brown or gray skin: **The *hippopotamus* lives in or near lakes or rivers in Africa.** [26]

ho·tel [hō·tel´] *n.* a place that rents rooms for sleeping and usually offers food: **We stayed in a *hotel* when we visited New York City.** [25]

Pronunciation Key

a	add	ō	open	th	thin
ā	ace	ô	off	th	this
â(r)	care	oi	oil	zh	vision
ä	palm	o͝o	took		
e	end	o͞o	pool	ə	a in about
ē	equal	ou	out		e in listen
i	it	u	up		i in pencil
ī	ice	û(r)	burn		o in melon
o	odd	yo͞o	use		u in circus

I

i·den·ti·fy [ī·den´tə·fī´] *v.,* **identified** to recognize or claim to be someone or something: **The witness *identified* the man in the lineup as the one who had robbed the store.** [12]

il·le·gal [i·lē´gəl] *adj.* against the law; not legal: **It is *illegal* to park your car in a no-parking zone.** *syn.* unlawful [31]

im·pa·tient [im·pā´shənt] *adj.* not willing to put up with delay; not patient: **Some of the people in the theater began to stamp their feet, *impatient* for the movie to begin.** [31]

im·po·lite [im´pə·līt´] *adj.* having bad manners; not polite: **Talking with food in your mouth is an *impolite* thing to do.** *syn.* rude [31]

im·por·tance [im·pôr´təns] *n.* the state of being important: **The doctor stressed the *importance* of proper exercise and plenty of rest.** [18]

im·por·tant [im·pôr´tənt] *adj.* deserving special attention or notice: **When you write a school report, it is *important* to organize your thoughts before you start to write.** [22]

im·pos·si·ble [im·pos´ə·bəl] *adj.* not able to be or to be done; not possible: **It is *impossible* for one person to be in two places at the same time.** [31]

im·pulse [im´puls] *n.* a sudden wish to act; a decision made without real thought: **He was on his way to work when on an *impulse* he decided to take the day off and go surfing.** [1]

im·pure [im·pyŏŏr´] *adj.* containing something unclean; not pure: **Some people use only bottled water because they believe water from the faucet is *impure*.** [31]

in·a·bil·i·ty [in´ə·bil´ə·tē] *n.* a lack of power or means to do something: **He wrote a letter to them apologizing for his *inability* to help with their problem.** [31]

in·com·plete [in´kəm·plēt´] *adj.* not finished; not complete: **Megan's report is *incomplete* because she still has to draw two maps for it.** [31]

in·cor·rect [in´kə·rekt´] *adj.* not correct or proper: **Each *incorrect* answer takes five points from the final score.** *syn.* wrong [31]

in·cred·i·ble [in·kred´ə·bəl] *adj.* hard to imagine: **In 1920, Babe Ruth had an *incredible* batting record; he hit more home runs by himself than any team in the league hit.** *syn.* amazing [31]

in·deed [in·dēd´] *adv.* in truth or in fact; really: **That senator is not really against the bill; *indeed,* he plans to vote for it.** [14]

in·def·i·nite [in·def´ə·nit] *adj.* not clear or exact; not definite: **He is planning to keep the rental car for an *indefinite* time because he is not sure when his own car will be repaired.** [31]

in·de·pen·dence [in´di·pen´dəns] *n.* the fact of being independent; freedom: **We celebrate the *independence* of our nation on the Fourth of July.** [18]

in·de·pen·dent [in´di·pen´dənt] *adj.* thinking or acting for oneself. **My baby sister is very *independent* and insists on feeding herself.** [31]

in·dex [in´deks] *n.* an alphabetical list at the end of a book that gives the numbers of the pages on which information about certain subjects can be found: **To find out if a book mentions a certain topic, look up the topic in the *index*.** [14]

In·di·an [in´dē·ən] *adj.* **1.** having to do with the American Indian people: **Navaho is an *Indian* language. 2.** having to do with the people of India: **In Asia, *Indian* women believe the color red is lucky.** [13]

in·di·ges·tion [in´də·jes´chən] *n.* an uncomfortable feeling that comes from eating the wrong things, eating too much, or eating too quickly: **I get *indigestion* from eating hot, spicy foods.** [31]

in·dus·try [in′dəs·trē] *n.*, **industries** the producing and selling of machine-made goods: **The making and selling of cars and trucks is one of the largest *industries* in this country.** [12]

in·ex·pen·sive [in′ik·spen′siv] *adj.* not expensive; not high in price: **These shoes were *inexpensive,* but they've lasted a long time.** *syn.* cheap [31]

in·for·mal [in·fôr′məl] *adj.* not formal; relaxed or casual: **Dad plays basketball in an *informal* league; the players don't wear team uniforms and no one keeps score.** [31]

in·ject [in·jekt′] *v.* to put in a comment or suggestion: **When any conversation seems to be getting too serious, she will always *inject* a little humor into it.** [33]

in·no·cent [in′ə·sənt] *adj.* free from doing wrong; not guilty: **The accused bank robbers said that they were completely *innocent* of the charges.** [22]

in·scrip·tion [in·skrip′shən] *n.* something that is written, carved, or marked on something: **We gave Mom a coffee mug with an *inscription* that said "To the World's Best Mom."** [32]

in·sert [in·sûrt′] *v.* to put or place in something: **Aunt Diane *inserts* the key into the lock and turns the key.** [4]

in·sist [in·sist′] *v.* to say or ask for something in a strong and forceful way: **Mom and Dad always *insist* that we wear our seat belts in the car.** [14]

in·spect [in·spekt′] *v.* to look at closely and carefully: **The workers *inspect* each new car before it leaves the factory to be sure that it is in good working condition.** [32]

in·spec·tor [in·spek′tər] *n.* a person whose job is to inspect something: **My cousin Louis is a building *inspector.*** [32]

in·stance [in′stəns] *n.* a single situation in which a general point is true: **Baseball is**

often a game played by men, but I know of at least one *instance* where a woman pitched and won a college game. *syns.* example, case [18]

in·stant [in′stənt] *adj.* without delay; immediate: **When our eyes met, there was *instant* recognition.** [22]

in·stinct [in′stingkt] *n.* an inner force that causes an animal to behave in a certain way: **Birds build their nests by *instinct.*** [14]

in·sur·ance [in·shŏŏr′əns] *n.* a way of protecting against the loss of money: **Some farmers have *insurance* that protects their property against loss from flooding.** [18]

in·tel·li·gence [in·tel′ə·jəns] *n.* the ability to use the mind to do such things as learn, understand, and remember: **Maria's ability to learn new things quickly is a sign of her *intelligence.*** [18]

in·tense [in·tens′] *adj.* very great or strong: **Not many people live in the Sahara because of the *intense* heat there.** *syn.* extreme [14]

in·ter·rupt [in′tə·rupt′] *v.* to stop or break in on someone or something: **Mom doesn't like it if we *interrupt* her while she is on the phone.** [33]

in·vis·i·ble [in·viz′ə·bəl] *adj.* not able to be seen; not visible: **Bacteria are so small that they are *invisible* without the aid of a microscope.** [31]

● ●

Pronunciation Key

a	add	ō	open	th	thin
ā	ace	ô	off	t͟h	this
â(r)	care	oi	oil	zh	vision
ä	palm	ŏŏ	took		
e	end	ōō	pool	ə	a in about
ē	equal	ou	out		e in listen
i	it	u	up		i in pencil
ī	ice	û(r)	burn		o in melon
o	odd	yōō	use		u in circus

● ●

ir·reg·u·lar [i·reg´yə·lər] *adj.* not usual or normal; not regular: *Run* is an *irregular* verb because the past tense is *ran*, not *runned*. [31]

J

joy·ful·ly [joi´fəl·lē] *adv.* in a happy way; with joy: **They *joyfully* greeted their granddaughter when she stepped off the plane.** [30]

L

lar·va [lär´və] *n.*, **larvae** an insect in an early stage of its life cycle: **Caterpillars are the *larvae* of butterflies or moths.** [26]

lat·er [lāt´ər] *adv.* coming after the usual or expected time: **We were supposed to meet at 7:30, but we arrived much *later*.** [10]

lat·ter [lat´ər] *n.* the second of two things that have just been mentioned: **Theodore Roosevelt and Franklin D. Roosevelt were cousins; the former was a Republican, and the *latter* was a Democrat.** [10]

launch [lônch] *v.* to put a boat or ship in the water, or send an aircraft, spacecraft, or rocket into the air: **NASA *launched* the first space shuttle in 1981.** [3]

lay·er [lā´ər] *n.* a single level or thickness of something: **She wore more than one *layer* of clothing to keep warm in the icy weather.** [13]

lead·er·ship [lē´dər·ship´] *n.* the condition of being a leader: **Teri was chosen as captain of the soccer team because she has outstanding qualities of *leadership*.** [19]

leg·is·la·tive [lej´is·lā´tiv] *adj.* having the power to make and pass laws: **Congress is the *legislative* branch of the U.S. government.** [27]

lift [lift] *v.* to raise into the air; pick up: **The man *lifted* his child to his shoulders so that she could look over the crowd to see the parade.** [16]

lin·en [lin´ən] *n.* a cloth made from the stalks of the flax plant: *Linen* **is a strong material, but it wrinkles easily.** [24]

li·quid [lik´wid] *n.* one of the three basic forms of matter; a substance that is not a gas or a solid: **A *liquid* such as water flows freely and will fit the shape of its container.** [1]

lo·cal [lō´kəl] *adj.* having to do with a certain place, especially the town or neighborhood one lives in: **She did the research for her report at the *local* public library. This newspaper carries foreign and national news stories in section A and *local* news in section B.** [15]

M

ma·jor·i·ty [mə·jôr´ə·tē] *n.* more than half: **The *majority* of Americans live in or near big cities.** [19]

mas·sive [mas´iv] *adj.* having great size; strong and heavy: **The entrance to the cave was blocked by a *massive* rock.** *syn.* huge [12]

mean-spir·it·ed [mēn´·spir´it id] *adj.* exhibiting or characterized by meanness of spirit: **The *mean-spirited* man often teased his neighbor's dog.** [8]

me·di·a [mē´dē·ə] *n.*, *pl.* the means of public communications, such as newspapers, television, and radio: **Candidates use the *media* to get their message to the public.** [26]

me·ter [mē´tər] *n.* a unit for measuring length: **A *meter* is equal to 39.37 inches.** [15]

mid·dle-aged [mid´(ə)l·ājd´] *adj.* not young and not old; of the age from about forty to sixty: **Many people think that anyone who is forty-five years old is *middle-aged*.** [8]

mis·chief [mis´chif] *n.* an act that is not truly bad but that causes some harm or damage: **Susie got into *mischief* when she smeared her mom's makeup all over her face.** [7]

mon·ster [mon´stər] *n.* a very large, imaginary creature with a frightening appearance: **When I was a little girl, I believed a *monster* lived under my bed.** [14]

moose [mo͞os] *n., pl.* **moose** [mo͞os] a large animal of the deer family, having a large head, long legs, and large slumped shoulders: **The male *moose* has wide, flat antlers.** [26]

mo·tive [mō´tiv] *n.* the reason for doing something: **Todd has been very friendly to everyone lately; I think his *motive* is that he wants us to vote for him for class president.** [15]

moun·tain [moun´tən] *n.* a large mass of land that rises high above the surrounding land: **Pikes Peak is a famous *mountain* in Colorado.** [3]

mum·my [mum´ē] *n.,* **mummies** a dead body that has been preserved to keep it from decaying: **In ancient Egypt, *mummies* were treated with natural solutions, wrapped in linen, and kept sealed in special tombs.** [12]

mu·si·cal [myo͞o´zi·kəl] *adj.* **1.** having to do with music: **A trumpet is a *musical* instrument. 2.** having a pleasant sound like music: **She had a pleasant, *musical* laugh.** [13]

mys·te·ri·ous [mis·tir´ē·əs] *adj.* hard to explain or understand; full of mystery: **Stonehenge is a *mysterious* rock formation in southern England; no one knows who built it or when or why they did so.** [27]

N

nat·u·ral·ly [nach´ər·əl·ē] *adv.* in a normal, natural way: **Do you find it hard to smile *naturally* when you're having your picture taken?** [30]

ne·ces·si·ty [nə·ses´ə·tē] *n.* something needed or required: **A good water supply is a *necessity* for any place where people live.** [19]

neg·a·tive [neg´ə·tiv] *adj.* **1.** saying or meaning no: **Shaking your head and turning your thumbs down are *negative* gestures. 2.** not helpful; not positive: **John has a *negative* attitude; he never wants to do what anyone else suggests.** [27]

ner·vous [nûr´vəs] *adj.* quick to become upset or excited; not relaxed: **She seems *nervous* when she speaks in front of the class.** *syn.* tense [4]

ner·vous·ly [nûr´vəs·lē] *adv.* in an uneasy way: **Norm shifted *nervously* in the batter's box as he waited for the pitcher to throw the ball.** [30]

New Year [n(y)o͞o´ yir´] *n.* the first day of a calendar year: **People often celebrate the *New Year* with a party the night before.** [8]

night·mare [nīt´mâr´] *n.* a frightening or disturbing dream: **My sister had a *nightmare* that there was a lion under her bed.** [4]

non·sense [non´sens´] *n.* talk or actions that have no meaning: **To me it sounds as if the baby is talking *nonsense*, but maybe it makes sense to him.** [1]

Pronunciation Key

a	add	ō	open	th	thin
ā	ace	ô	off	t͟h	this
â(r)	care	oi	oil	zh	vision
ä	palm	o͝o	took		
e	end	o͞o	pool	ə	a in about
ē	equal	ou	out		e in listen
i	it	u	up		i in pencil
ī	ice	û(r)	burn		o in melon
o	odd	yo͞o	use		u in circus

nov·el [nov´əl] *n.* a written story that is long enough to fill a book: **A *novel* may be based on real events, but it is made up by its author.** [24]

nu·cle·us [n(y)o͞o´klē·əs] *n.,* **nuclei** [n(y)o͞o´klē·ī] the central part of an atom: **Negatively charged electrons revolve around the *nucleus* of an atom. The *nuclei* of atoms have a positive electrical charge.** [26]

O

o·be·di·ence [ō·bē´dē·əns] *n.* the fact of doing what one is told or is supposed to do: ***Obedience* to one's parents is expected of a child.** [18]

ob·ject [əb·jekt´] *v.* to be against: **Dad *objected* to our eating in the car.** *syn.* oppose [33]

ob·jec·tion [əb·jek´shən] *n.* the act of objecting, or a reason for objecting: **Robert calmly gave his *objections* to the plans.** [33]

ob·vi·ous [ob´vē·əs] *adj.* easy to see or understand: **Her smile made it *obvious* that she was having a good time.** *syns.* plain, clear [27]

oc·cu·py [ok´yə·pī] *v.,* **occupied 1.** to take up the space of: **That apartment is *occupied* by the Smith family.** *syn.* fill **2.** to take up the interest of: **During the long plane flight, she *occupied* herself with a book.** [12]

op·po·nent [ə·pō´nənt] *n.* a person or group on the other side in a contest: **Melissa defeated her *opponent* in the tennis match.** [22]

o·rig·i·nal [ə·rij´ə·nəl] *adj.* having to do with the earliest or first: **New York and Virginia were among the *original* thirteen states of the United States.** [13]

or·phan [ôr´fən] *n.* a child whose parents are dead: **The *orphan* was raised by his aunt.** [25]

o·val [ō´vəl] *adj.* shaped like an egg: **The running track at our school has an *oval* shape.** [25]

own·er·ship [ō´nər·ship´] *n.* the fact of owning something: **This paper proves her *ownership* of the car.** [30]

P

pal·ace [pal´is] *n.* a large and grand building that is the official home of a king, queen, or other ruler: **The Queen of England lives in a huge *palace* in London.** [24]

part·ner·ship [pärt´nər·ship´] *n.* the condition of being a partner; a business that is run by partners: **Pat and her brother have a *partnership* in a bakery.** [19]

peace·ful·ly [pēs´fəl·ē] *adv.* in a peaceful way; without fighting or trouble: **The United Nations is working to see that the dispute between the two countries is settled *peacefully*.** *syn.* calmly [30]

peach [pēch] *n.* a sweet, juicy fruit with a fuzzy skin and a hard pit: **The *peach* grows in warm parts of the world.** [2]

per·ma·nent [pûr´mən·ənt] *adj.* lasting or meant to last for a long time without change: **After visiting England several times, he liked the country so much that he decided to become a *permanent* resident.** *syns.* lasting, enduring [22]

per·son·al·i·ty [pûr´sən·al´ə·tē] *n.* all the habits, feelings, and other traits that show what a person is like: **Everyone likes Michelle because she has a nice, friendly *personality*.** [19]

pier [pir] *n.* a structure built out over the water from the shore: **A *pier* is used as a dock for boats and as a walkway.** [7]

pil·low [pil´ō] *n.* a cushion that is filled with soft materials and used to support the head: **People put their head on a *pillow* while they sleep.** [14]

plat·form [plat´fôrm´] *n.* a flat surface raised above the ground: **The band was seated on a *platform* in front of the dance floor.** [25]

pleas·ant [plez´ənt] *adj.* pleasing to the mind or senses: **It was nice and sunny, and we had a *pleasant* day at the beach.** [24]

point·ed [poin´tid] *adj.* clearly directed or aimed at: **Her *pointed* question about my activities took me by surprise.** [16]

po·lit·i·cal [pə·lit´·i·kəl] *adj.* having to do with the activities of government: **There are two major *political* parties in the United States, the Democrats and the Republicans.** [13]

pos·i·tive [poz´ə·tiv] *adj.* absolutely sure; with no doubt: **I'm *positive* that I'm right, because I checked the facts in an encyclopedia.** *syn.* certain [27]

pound [pound] *n.* a unit for measuring weight: **There are 2,000 *pounds* in a short ton.** [3]

praise [prāz] *n.* words showing approval of someone or something: **The teacher gave Ben's report a lot of *praise*.** [2]

pre·fer [pri·fûr´] *v.,* **preferred** to like one thing or person better than another: **We offered them a ride home, but they said they *preferred* to walk because it was such a nice day.** [16]

pre·scribe [pri·skrīb´] *v.,* **prescribed** to order a certain medicine or treatment for a patient: **When I had the flu, the doctor *prescribed* bed rest and a very light diet.** [32]

pres·ence [prez´əns] *n.* the fact of being in a certain place: **A smoke detector acts to sense the *presence* of a fire in a room.** [18]

pres·i·dent [prez´ə·dənt] *n.* the highest-ranking official in a country or group: **The *president* of a college is in charge of how it is run.** [22]

prime [prīm] *adj.* first in value or importance: ***Prime* beef is meat of very high quality.** [2]

pris·on [priz´(ə)n] *n.* a place in which people found guilty of a crime must stay for a certain period of time: **They are in *prison* for armed robbery.** [24]

prof·it [prof´it] *n.* any money that a business has left after its expenses have been paid: **Sales were good last year, and the firm made a *profit*.** [24]

pro·ject [prə·jekt´] *v.* to plan or propose: **We *projected* an increase in funds for the library.** [33]

pro·jec·tion [prə·jek´shən] *n.* an estimate of a future outcome: **Their *projections* show that our community will need a new high school within ten years.** [33]

proof [pro͞of] *n.* a certain way to show that something is true: **A driver's license is *proof* that you have passed a test and may drive a car.** [3]

purse [pûrs] *n.* a bag used to carry money, keys, cosmetics, and other small personal items: **Joanne carries her *purse* from a strap over one shoulder.** *syns.* handbag, pocketbook [4]

Q

qual·i·fy [kwol´ə·fī] *v.,* **qualified** to be suitable or fit, as for a job or privilege: **After Toni won her first two races, she *qualified* for the finals.** [12]

Pronunciation Key

a	add	ō	open	th	thin
ā	ace	ô	off	th	this
â(r)	care	oi	oil	zh	vision
ä	palm	o͝o	took		
e	end	o͞o	pool	ə	a in about
ē	equal	ou	out		e in listen
i	it	u	up		i in pencil
ī	ice	û(r)	burn		o in melon
o	odd	yo͞o	use		u in circus

R

ra·di·us [rā´dē·əs] *n., pl.* **ra·di·i** [rā´dē·ī] **1.** any line going from the center to the outside edge of a circle or sphere: **The spoke of a bicycle wheel is a *radius*. 2.** the shorter, thicker bone of the lower arm: **She broke the *radius* in her right arm when she fell from the top of the slide.** [26]

rap·id [rap´id] *adj.* very fast; with great speed: **She made a *rapid* recovery from her illness and was back in school in two days.** [1]

ra·zor [rā´zər] *n.* a small tool with a sharp blade used to remove hair from the face or body: **My older brother uses an electric *razor* to shave.** [15]

re·ac·tion [rē·ak´shən] *n.* an action in response to something else that happened or was done: **What was Mom's *reaction* when you told her you had lost your house key?** [28]

read·er [rē´dər] *n.* a person who reads: **She finished the book in two days because she's a fast *reader*.** [13]

re·ceive [ri·sēv´] *v.* to get or take what is given: **I'm sure Grandma will *receive* lots of cards on her birthday.** [7]

re·ceiv·er [ri·sē´vər] *n.* a person or thing that receives something: **A player who catches passes in football is a pass *receiver*. A television *receiver* can get broadcast signals through a cable.** [7]

re·con·struc·tion [rē´kən·struk´shən] *n.* the act of building again: **The time after a war is often known as *reconstruction*, a period when the defeated country is restored to its former condition.** [28]

re·fer [ri·fûr´] *v.,* **referring** to direct attention to: **When you said "Lee," were you *referring* to the son or to his father?** [16]

rein [rān] *n.* a narrow strap fastened to a horse's bit that is used by the driver or rider to control the horse: **The horse responded quickly to just a light touch on the *reins*.** [7]

re·ject [ri·jekt´] *v.* to refuse to use: **The committee can *reject* any plan that does not fit its budget. He *rejected* our offer to help with the work and said he would do it all by himself.** [33]

re·la·tion·ship [ri·lā´shən·ship´] *n.* the condition of being connected to some other person or thing: **Carmen has a good working *relationship* with her boss.** [30]

re·lief [ri·lēf´] *n.* something that brings freedom from suffering or sorrow: **Sarah took medicine to provide some *relief* from her cold.** [7]

re·new·al [ri·n(y)ōō´əl] *n.* the act of making something new or as if new again: **Spring brings a sense of *renewal* to the land.** [28]

re·pay·ment [ri·pā´mənt] *n.* the act of paying something back: **The bank set up a monthly schedule for the *repayment* of the car loan.** [28]

re·place·ment [ri·plās´mənt] *n.* the act of replacing or being replaced: **The radio did not work, so the store gave us a free *replacement* for it.** [28]

re·pro·duc·tion [rē´prə·duk´shən] *n.* something made from an original; something produced again: **We saw a famous painting by Monet and bought a poster that was a *reproduction* of it.** *syn.* copy [28]

re·spec·tive·ly [ri·spek´tiv·lē] *adv.* in the order given: **You, Mom, and I are sitting in Row 3; we have seats 3A, 3B, and 3C, *respectively*.** [30]

re·spon·si·bil·i·ty [ri·spon´sə·bil´ə·tē] *n.* the condition of being responsible for: **Filling the cats' water bowl is Charlie's *responsibility*, and giving them food is mine.** [19]

re·turn [ri·tûrn´] *v.* to take, bring, or send back: **I *returned* the shirt Aunt Sandy sent me for my birthday because it was too small.** [16]

re·ward [ri·wôrd´] *n.* something won or gotten in return for some work or service: **Steve received a ten-dollar *reward* for returning a lost wallet to its owner.** [4]

ri·val [rī′vəl] *n.* someone who tries to do something better than another person: **The American figure skater scored just enough points to defeat her** *rival* **from Japan.** *syns.* foe, opponent —*v.* to try to win or defeat: **The two top teams** *rival* **each other for the pennant.** [15]

roar [rôr] *v.* to make a very loud, deep noise: **The plane's engines** *roar* **as the pilot increases the speed to take off.** [4]

roast [rōst] *v.* to cook food in an oven or over hot coals: **Dad will** *roast* **a turkey for dinner.** [2]

Ro·man [rō′mən] *adj.* having to do with Rome: **The** *Roman* **army conquered much of the ancient world.** [13]

rot·ten [rot′(ə)n] *adj.* **1.** spoiled and decayed; not fit to be used or eaten: **The** *rotten* **potatoes had a very bad smell. 2.** unpleasant or disagreeable: **It is best to avoid a person who has a** *rotten* **temper.** [13]

rough [ruf] *adj.* not smooth or even; hard to deal with: **It was a** *rough* **situation for the puppies when their mother died.** [6]

ru·mor [rōō′mər] *n.* a story that is being passed around from person to person, and that seems true without any proof: **We heard** *rumors* **that the principal is leaving our school at the end of this year.** [3]

rup·ture [rup′chər] *v.* to break open: **If that pipe should ever** *rupture,* **the whole building would be flooded.** [33]

S

sack [sak] *n.* a paper or plastic container to carry things: **She brought her lunch to school in a brown paper** *sack.* *syn.* bag [1]

salm·on [sam′ən] *n., pl.* **salm·on** [sam′ən] a large, silver-colored fish whose meat is used for food: *Salmon* **live in the ocean but return to fresh water to lay eggs.** [26]

salt [sôlt] *n.* a white crystal that is mined from the earth or taken from sea water: *Salt* **is often used to season and preserve food.** [3]

Sat·urn [sat′ərn] *n.* the planet in our solar system that is sixth farthest from the sun: **The rings of** *Saturn* **are made up of particles of ice and water.** [25]

sau·cer [sô′sər] *n.* a small, shallow dish that a cup sits on: **When she stirred her coffee, it spilled over onto the** *saucer.* [3]

scarce [skârs] *adj.* hard to find or get; not common: **Fresh raspberries are** *scarce* **at this time of year, so they're very expensive.** *syn.* rare [4]

sce·nic [sē′nik *or* sen′ik] *adj.* having to do with a beautiful place or area: **The** *scenic* **highway along the Pacific Coast has the ocean on one side and the mountains on the other.** [15]

scrib·ble [skrib′əl] *v.,* **scribbled** to draw or write in a sloppy way: **Jimmy** *scribbled* **on the wall with a crayon, and Dad was really upset.** [32]

scribe [skrīb] *n.* a person who wrote or copied books by hand at the time in history before printing was invented: **In the Middle Ages not many people knew how to write, and a** *scribe* **was an important person.** [32]

•••••••••••••••••••••••••••••••••••

Pronunciation Key

a	add	ō	open	th	thin
ā	ace	ô	off	th	this
â(r)	care	oi	oil	zh	vision
ä	palm	ŏŏ	took		
e	end	ōō	pool	ə	a in about
ē	equal	ou	out		e in listen
i	it	u	up		i in pencil
ī	ice	û(r)	burn		o in melon
o	odd	yōō	use		u in circus

•••••••••••••••••••••••••••••••••••

script [skript] *n.* the written lines of a play, movie, television show, or other spoken performance: **The actor read the *script* for a new play and agreed to take the part.** [32]

scrub [skrub] *v.*, **scrubbed** to rub hard or roughly, as in cleaning something: **He *scrubbed* the rug to remove the mud stains.** [16]

sea·shore [sē´shôr´] *n.* the place where the land and the sea meet: **The *seashore* is flat and sandy all along this beach.** [8]

sen·si·tive [sen´sə·tiv] *adj.* capable of feeling, reacting, or appreciating quickly: **A baby is very *sensitive* to loud sounds.** [27]

ser·vant [sûr´vənt] *n.* a person whose regular job is to work for another person, doing such things as cleaning, cooking, laundry, and the like: **In the past, many wealthy families employed a butler who acted as the head *servant* of their household.** [22]

shout [shout] *v.* to call out loudly: **Did Tony *shout* and wave his arms to get their attention?** *syn.* yell [3]

sig·ni·fi·cant [sig·nif´ə·kənt] *adj.* having special meaning: **She and her husband first met on Valentine's Day, so February 14 has become a *significant* day for them.** *syn.* important [22]

si·ren [sī´rən] *n.* a device that makes a loud, shrill noise as a warning: **The sound of a *siren* filled the air as the fire truck raced to the fire.** [24]

sketch [skech] *v.* to draw: **Using charcoal, I will *sketch* an outline of the castle.** [1]

sleigh [slā] *n.* a carriage on runners like a sled that is used to travel over snow and ice: **A *sleigh* is often pulled by horses.** [6]

slice [slīs] *v.* to cut into thin, flat sections: **The chef will *slice* the roast beef for the diners.** [2]

slope [slōp] *n.* a surface that is not flat or level: **She moved at high speed down the ski *slope*.** [2]

soar [sôr] *v.* to fly high with little effort: **An eagle can *soar* high above the earth by riding on currents of air.** [9]

so-called [sō´kôld´] *adj.* called such, but not so: **Hank should know that his *so-called* friend is going around saying bad things about him.** [8]

sore [sôr] *adj.* causing pain: **Les could not put his shoe on over his *sore* toe.** *syn.* hurt [9]

source [sôrs] *n.* the place or thing that something comes from: **A small lake in Minnesota is the *source* of the Mississippi River.** *syn.* origin [4]

spar·kling [spär´kling] *adj.* effervescent; bubbly: **Holly's *sparkling* personality attracted others to her.** [4]

speak [spēk´] *v.* to use words to express one's thoughts: **Tana has been *speaking* in sentences since she was about two years old.** *syn.* talk [16]

speak·er [spē´kər] *n.* a person who makes a speech: **The *speaker* stepped to the microphone, and the audience grew quiet.** [13]

spe·cies [spē´shēz *or* spē´sēz] *n.* a group of plants or animals with shared features that separate them from others: **The dog, the wolf, and the fox are different *species* of the same family.** [26]

spec·ta·cle [spek´tə·kəl] *n.* an unusual sight that is very impressive: **The Fourth of July fireworks display was quite a *spectacle*.** [32]

spec·tac·u·lar [spek·tak´yə·lər] *adj.* very unusual or impressive; sure to be remembered: **The view of New York City from the top of the World Trade Center is a *spectacular* sight.** [32]

spec·ta·tor [spek´tā·tər] *n.* a person who watches a particular event: **Hours before the parade began, *spectators* began to line the downtown streets.** [32]

spec·trum [spek´trəm] *n.* the bands of color in a rainbow: **The colors of the *spectrum* are red, orange, yellow, green, blue, indigo, and violet.** [32]

spell·ing [spel´ing] *n.* the act of putting letters together to form words: **Kristy likes to learn the correct *spelling* for unusual words.**—*adj.* relating to the school subject: **Amy got nine out of ten words correct on the *spelling* test.** [16]

spike [spīk] *n.* a sharp, pointed object: **A railroad *spike* is a large piece of metal used to hold a track in place.** [2]

spi·ral [spī´rəl] *adj.* curving or winding: **A *spiral* staircase in the theater connected the lobby to the balcony level.** [24]

splen·did [splen´did] *adj.* very impressive or very good: **Every time we eat in that restaurant, the food is absolutely *splendid.*** *syns.* magnificent, excellent [1]

squeeze [skwēz] *v.* to press the parts or sides of something together; force by pressing: **My father likes to *squeeze* fresh oranges to get orange juice every morning.** [2]

stake [stāk] *n.* a stick with a pointed end that is stuck in the ground to support something: **A tomato plant will grow along the ground unless a *stake* holds it up.** [9]

state·ment [stāt´mənt] *n.* a formal comment on something that has happened: **The police wrote down what the witness said and then asked her to sign a *statement.*** [19]

steak [stāk] *n.* a slice of meat or fish that is good for broiling, grilling, or frying: **For dinner, Dad is going to cook a *steak* on the outdoor grill.** [9]

steal [stēl] *v.* to take something that belongs to another without permission: **I told John it is against the law to *steal* a car; besides, he could borrow mine.** [9]

steel [stēl] *n.* a strong, hard metal that is a mixture of iron and carbon: ***Steel* is used to make cars, tools, and machines.** [9]

stim·u·lus [stim´yə·ləs] *n.,* **stimuli** [stim´yə·lī] something that causes a reaction: **Light is a *stimulus* for plants. Living things are affected by such *stimuli* as heat and light.** [26]

straight [strāt] *adj.* not curved: **Highway 10 is a *straight* road across the desert with no hills or turns.**—*adv.* going in an even way in one direction: **I was told to go *straight* to bed.** [6]

stretch·er [strech´ər] *n.* a sort of frame or simple bed on which a sick or injured person is carried: **The player who was injured during the game was taken off the field on a *stretcher.*** [13]

stroke [strōk] *v.* to pass the hand over gently; to pet: **Use a light touch when you *stroke* the kitten.** [2]

sub·scrip·tion [səb·skrip´shən] *n.* an agreement to pay for a certain number of newspapers, magazines, tickets, and so on: **Mom has a *subscription* to a newsmagazine that comes in the mail every week.** [32]

suc·cess·ful·ly [sək·ses´fəl·ē] *adv.* having or getting a good result; with success: **If the plan goes *successfully,* the company will gain a lot of new business.** [30]

suf·fi·cient [sə·fish´ənt] *adj.* just as much as is wanted or needed: **In order for garden plants to grow well, they need a *sufficient* amount of water and sunlight.** *syn.* enough [22]

●●●●●●●●●●●●●●●●●●●●●●●●●●●●●

Pronunciation Key

a	add	ō	open	th	thin
ā	ace	ô	off	th	this
â(r)	care	oi	oil	zh	vision
ä	palm	o͝o	took		
e	end	o͞o	pool	ə	a in about
ē	equal	ou	out		e in listen
i	it	u	up		i in pencil
ī	ice	û(r)	burn		o in melon
o	odd	yo͞o	use		u in circus

●●●●●●●●●●●●●●●●●●●●●●●●●●●●●

sum·mit [sum´it] *n.* the highest point or level: **We climbed to the** *summit* **of the mountain.** [1]

sup·ply [sə·plī´] *n.,* **supplies** food and other necessary items: **The hikers carried their** *supplies* **in packs on their backs.** [12]

sus·pect [sə·spekt´] *v.* **1.** to think someone is guilty without actual proof: **The police** *suspect* **that one of the guards let the robbers into the bank. 2.** to believe that something is true or possible: **I** *suspect* **that we will have a quiz in math class tomorrow.** [32]

sus·pense [sə·spens´] *n.* a state of uncertainty in which one does not know what will happen next: **Very often, mystery movies keep viewers in** *suspense* **right up to the very end.** [25]

sys·tem [sis´təm] *n.* a certain way to do something: **The company uses a computerized** *system* **to keep track of how much money it spends.** [6]

T

tal·ent [tal´ənt] *n.* a natural or inborn ability to do something: **She showed great** *talent* **as an actress from the time she began in movies as a young girl.** [24]

teen·a·ger [tēn´a´jər] *n.* a person between the ages of thirteen and nineteen: **Nick likes to listen to rock music now that he is a** *teenager.* [8]

thief [thēf] *n.,* **thieves** [thēvz] a person who steals: **The** *thieves* **stole the car from the driveway.** [7]

thigh [thī] *n.* the upper part of the leg between the hip and the knee: **I hurt a muscle in my** *thigh.* [2]

though [thō] *conj.* even if: **Martha really doesn't like to cook,** *though* **she does like to bake.** *syn.* although [6]

thought·ful·ly [thôt´fəl·ē] *adv.* showing concern for other people: **He** *thoughtfully* **kept his radio very low so he wouldn't disturb his sister.** [30]

thou·sand [thou´zənd] *n.* the number that is ten times one hundred; 1,000: *Thousands* **of motorists were stranded during the blizzard.** [3]

threat·en [thret´(ə)n] *v.* to put in danger; menace: **The strong winds** *threatened* **to overturn the small boat.** [16]

thun·der·storm [thun´dər·stôrm´] *n.* a storm with thunder and lightning: **The flashes of lightning and crashes of thunder frighten our dog Max during a** *thunderstorm.* [8]

to·ken [tō´kən] *n.* a small thing that stands for another thing that is larger or greater: **This gift certificate is a** *token* **of my appreciation for your kindness.** [24]

tran·script [tran´skript´] *n.* a written copy of something: **I have two** *transcripts* **of my high school record since I moved from Utah to Ohio during that time.** [32]

trea·son [trē´zən] *n.* the crime of betraying one's country: **Giving military secrets of one's country to the enemy is an act of** *treason.* [24]

tre·men·dous [tri·men´dəs] *adj.* extremely large, strong, or great: **Growing boys are said to have** *tremendous* **appetites.** [27]

trout [trout] *n., s.* or *pl.* a fish found in cool, fresh waters: *Trout* **are often seen swimming in brooks and streams.** [26]

tur·tle [tûr´təl] *n.* a reptile with a low, flat body covered by a round, hard shell: **The** *turtle* **pulls its head and feet into its shell for protection.** [4]

U

un·com·fort·a·ble [un·kum´fər·tə·bəl] *adj.* not comfortable: **They were *uncomfortable* on the plane because their seats were so narrow.** [28]

un·em·ploy·ment [un´im·ploi´mənt] *n.* the fact of being without a job: **Every month the government releases *unemployment* figures that tell how many people are jobless and looking for work.** [28]

un·ex·pect·ed·ly [un´ik·spek´tid·lē] *adv.* coming or happening without notice; not expected: **A storm came up *unexpectedly*, and we got soaking wet.** [28]

un·for·tu·nate·ly [un·fôr´chə·nit´lē] *adv.* without luck: **Robert *unfortunately* got on the wrong bus and ended up on the other side of town.** [28]

un·like·ly [un·līk´lē] *adj.* not probable or true: **It is possible that there is life on the planet Mars, but I would say it's highly *unlikely*.** [28]

un·pre·dict·a·ble [un´pri·dik´tə·bəl] *adj.* not able to be known in advance: **That football team is very *unpredictable*; in one game they play well and win, and then in the next game they lose badly.** [28]

un·suc·cess·ful [un´sək·ses´fəl] *adj.* not having a good result: **The movie was *unsuccessful* and lost millions of dollars at the box office.** [28]

un·u·su·al·ly [un·yo͞o´zho͞o·əl·ē] *adv.* not ordinarily; not in the usual way: **The flowers are already starting to bloom because of our *unusually* warm weather.** [28]

up·right [up´rīt´] *adj.* straight up; not bent: **Grandma always scolded me for not sitting *upright*.** *syn.* erect [8]

V

va·ried [vâr´ēd] *adj.* having many forms or types: **The *varied* colors of the leaves are beautiful in the fall.** *syn.* differing [12]

var·i·ous [vâr´ē·əs] *adj.* not like each other: **The rose grows in *various* colors, such as red, pink, yellow, and white.** *syn.* different [27]

vel·vet [vel´vit] *n.* a kind of cloth with a smooth, very soft and thick surface: **His gray wool coat has a collar of black *velvet*.**—*adj.* relating to the kind of fabric: **She dreamed of one day owning a *velvet* dress with enormous ribbons.** [14]

vi·tal [vīt´(ə)l] *adj.* very important or necessary: **She is *vital* to the team's success, and it would be hard for them to win without her.** *syn.* essential [15]

W

war·rant [wôr´ənt] *n.* an official order in writing that gives a person authority to do something: **The police cannot search a person's home without a search *warrant*.** [4]

● ●

Pronunciation Key

a	add	ō	open	th	thin
ā	ace	ô	off	t̶h̶	this
â(r)	care	oi	oil	zh	vision
ä	palm	o͝o	took		
e	end	o͞o	pool	ə	a in about
ē	equal	ou	out		e in listen
i	it	u	up		i in pencil
ī	ice	û(r)	burn		o in melon
o	odd	yo͞o	use		u in circus

● ●

weak [wēk] *adj.* not strong; lacking the needed power or energy: **After he was sick and did not eat for a few days, he felt very** *weak.* [9]

weap·on [wep´ən] *n.* any tool or device that is used for attack or defense: **A machine gun is a type of** *weapon.* [24]

weath·er [weth´ər] *n.* the condition of the outside air at a certain time and place: **The** *weather* **has been especially cold this winter.** [9]

week [wēk] *n.* a period of seven days, especially beginning with Sunday and ending with Saturday: **He works five days each** *week.* [9]

weigh [wā] *v.* to find out how heavy something is: **The butcher** *weighed* **the meat on his scale.** [7]

wheth·er [hweth´er or weth´er] *conj.* if it is likely that: **Let me know** *whether* **or not you can go to the party.** *syn.* if [9]

won·der [wun´dər] *v.* to want to know about: **I've often** *wondered* **what happened to our cat after it ran away.** [16]

won·der·ful·ly [wun´dər·fəl·ē] *adv.* in a wonderful way: **The sun was** *wonderfully* **warm today.** [30]

worse [wûrs] *adj.* the comparative form of bad: **They beat us 3-0 in the first game, and the second game was even** *worse;* **we lost 5-0.** [4]

Y

young [yung] *adj.* not old: **A three-year-old is a** *young* **child.** [6]

youth [yōōth] *n.* **1.** the time of life between early childhood and adulthood: **Grandpa tells great stories about his** *youth* **in Ireland. 2.** a young man: **He left there when he was just a** *youth.* [3]

Your Word Logs

This is a special place where you can keep track of words that are important to you.

Lesson Word Log

pages 106–111

This is the place for you to list words you need to study. List the words from any lesson that need your special attention. Then they'll be easy to find when you're ready to study them. There's a page for each unit of your spelling book.

Personal Word Log

pages 112–118

You choose the words to list on these pages. It's up to you! Include new words, words that are especially interesting, and any other words you want to remember. Group the words into categories any way you like, and write them on these pages.

➤ words from other languages
➤ vivid words
➤ craft words
➤ food words
➤ tricky words
➤ big words
➤ music words
➤ art words
➤ science and math words
➤ social studies words
➤ words you would like to use when you write
➤ words you are curious about
➤ words you have trouble pronouncing
➤ technical words like computer words and business words

Unit 1 : Lesson Word Log

List the words you missed on the pretest. It's a good idea to include other words from the lesson that you aren't sure you can spell correctly.

LESSON 1

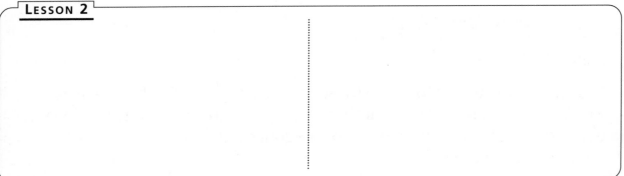

LESSON 2

LESSON 3

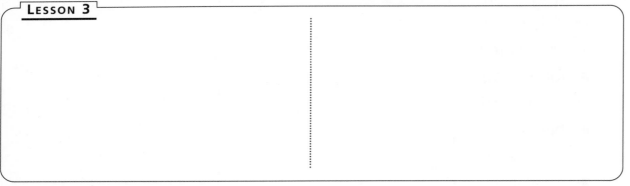

LESSON 4

ELEMENTS OF LANGUAGE | Introductory Course | *Spelling*

Unit 2: Lesson Word Log

List the words you missed on the pretest. It's a good idea to include other words from the lesson that you aren't sure you can spell correctly.

LESSON 6

LESSON 7

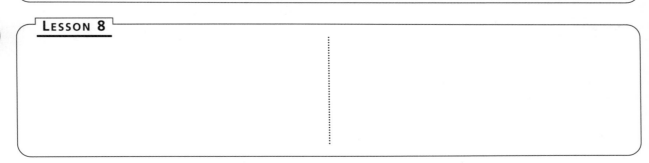

LESSON 8

LESSON 9

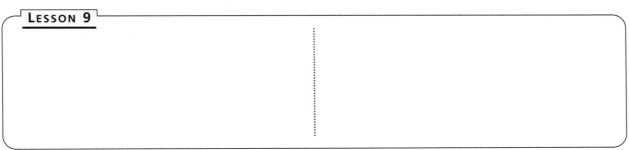

LESSON 10

Unit 3: Lesson Word Log

List the words you missed on the pretest. It's a good idea to include other words from the lesson that you aren't sure you can spell correctly.

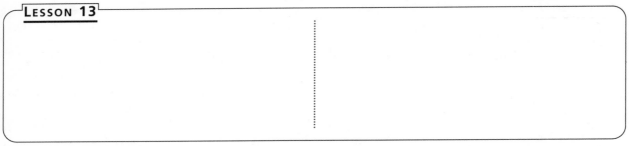

LESSON 12

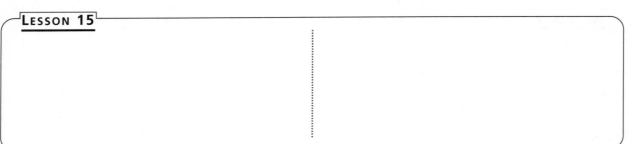

LESSON 13

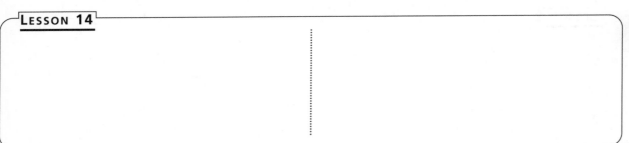

LESSON 14

LESSON 15

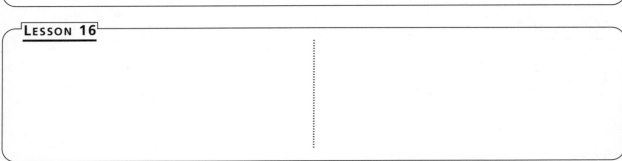

LESSON 16

ELEMENTS OF LANGUAGE | Introductory Course | *Spelling*

Unit 4: Lesson Word Log

List the words you missed on the pretest. It's a good idea to include other words from the lesson that you aren't sure you can spell correctly.

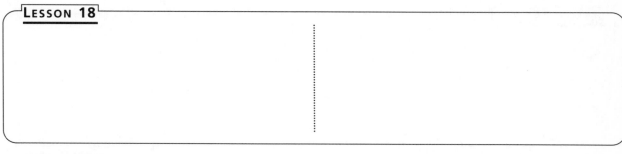

LESSON 18

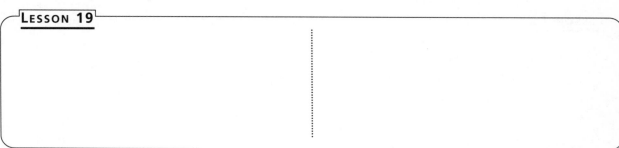

LESSON 19

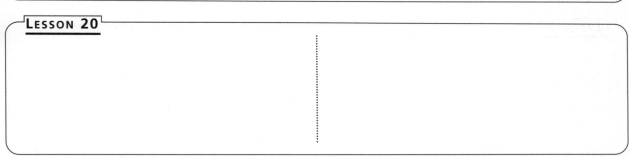

LESSON 20

LESSON 21

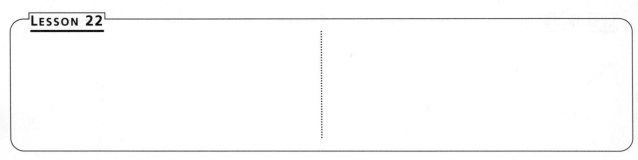

LESSON 22

Unit 5: Lesson Word Log

List the words you missed on the pretest. It's a good idea to include other words from the lesson that you aren't sure you can spell correctly.

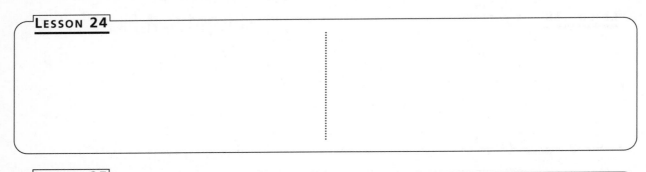

LESSON 24

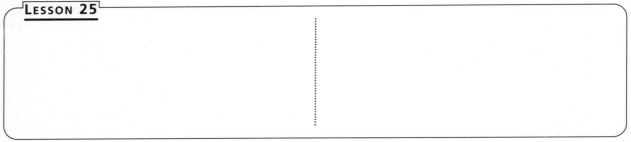

LESSON 25

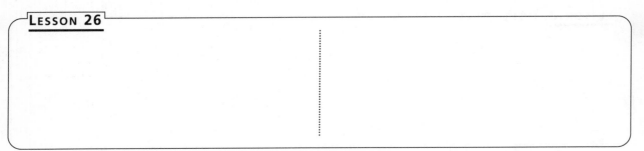

LESSON 26

LESSON 27

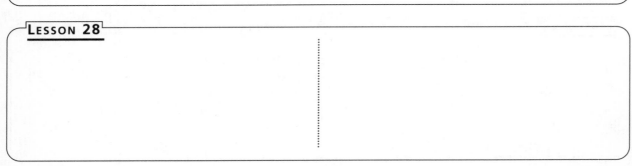

LESSON 28

Unit 6: Lesson Word Log

List the words you missed on the pretest. It's a good idea to include other words from the lesson that you aren't sure you can spell correctly.

LESSON 30

LESSON 31

LESSON 32

LESSON 33

Personal Word Log

You choose the words to list on these pages. It's up to you! Include new words, words that are especially interesting, and any other words you want to remember.

WORD AND NOTES

WORD AND NOTES

WORD AND NOTES

WORD AND NOTES

WORD AND NOTES

Personal Word Log

You choose the words to list on these pages. It's up to you! Include new words, words that are especially interesting, and any other words you want to remember.

WORD AND NOTES	

WORD AND NOTES	

WORD AND NOTES	

WORD AND NOTES	

WORD AND NOTES	

Personal Word Log

You choose the words to list on these pages. It's up to you! Include new words, words that are especially interesting, and any other words you want to remember.

> **WORD AND NOTES**

> **WORD AND NOTES**

> **WORD AND NOTES**

> **WORD AND NOTES**

> **WORD AND NOTES**

Personal Word Log

You choose the words to list on these pages. It's up to you! Include new words, words that are especially interesting, and any other words you want to remember.

WORD AND NOTES

WORD AND NOTES

WORD AND NOTES

WORD AND NOTES

WORD AND NOTES

Personal Word Log

You choose the words to list on these pages. It's up to you! Include new words, words that are especially interesting, and any other words you want to remember.

WORD AND NOTES

WORD AND NOTES

WORD AND NOTES

WORD AND NOTES

WORD AND NOTES

Personal Word Log

You choose the words to list on these pages. It's up to you! Include new words, words that are especially interesting, and any other words you want to remember.

┌─ **WORD AND NOTES** ───┐
│   │
│   │
│   │
│   │
└──┘

┌─ **WORD AND NOTES** ───┐
│   │
│   │
│   │
│   │
└──┘

┌─ **WORD AND NOTES** ───┐
│   │
│   │
│   │
│   │
└──┘

┌─ **WORD AND NOTES** ───┐
│   │
│   │
│   │
│   │
└──┘

┌─ **WORD AND NOTES** ───┐
│   │
│   │
│   │
│   │
└──┘

Personal Word Log

You choose the words to list on these pages. It's up to you! Include new words, words that are especially interesting, and any other words you want to remember.

WORD AND NOTES	

WORD AND NOTES	

WORD AND NOTES	

WORD AND NOTES	

WORD AND NOTES	